BEAST

BEAST

Tendai Mtawarira

with Andy Capostagno

MACMILLAN

First published in 2019
by Pan Macmillan South Africa
Private Bag X19
Northlands
Johannesburg
2116

www.panmacmillan.co.za

ISBN 978-1-77010-653-6
e-ISBN 978-1-77010-654-3

Editing by Sean Fraser
Proofreading by Wesley Thompson
Indexing by Christopher Merrett
Design and typesetting by Triple M Design, Johannesburg
Cover design by publicide
Cover and author photographs by Steve Haag

Printed by **novus print**, a division of Novus Holdings

CONTENTS

ABOUT THE AUTHOR

Andy Capostagno has been talking about Beast for 17 years. Best known for his rugby, cricket and hockey commentary with SuperSport, Andy was also the rugby correspondent for the *Mail & Guardian* for a quarter of a century. *Beast* is his fifth book, following *Jonty in Pictures*; *Memorable Moments in One-Day Cricket*; *Fancourt: The Road to the Presidents Cup* and *Ystervarkrivier: A Slice of Life*.

PREFACE

Summer is clinging on tight in Durban. It's 34 degrees and uncomfortable in a way that only Durban can be. They say the suicide rate triples in the city in January and February and even the palm trees seem sick of the enervating mix of heat and humidity. Rugby, as it was conceived by William Webb Ellis and his colleagues at Rugby School, was not meant to be played in this weather. But out on the training field next to Kings Park, the Sharks players are being put through their paces by the coaching staff.

Among the rising Springbok stars such as S'bu Nkosi and Thomas du Toit, the hero of our story plies his trade, hitting tackle bags, straining the giant rubber bands with his power and casting an experienced eye over the youngsters. Tendai 'Beast' Mtawarira is not far short of his 34th birthday, but he looks a decade younger.

He has broad shoulders and a narrow waist, attributes that are usually reversed in prop forwards at club level. His massive thighs and biceps speak of a life spent in the gym, while his jutting black beard softens the contours of his lantern jaw. There is a burning intensity to his gaze, but he smiles broadly and laughs easily.

Beast is coming to the end of a remarkable career. Along the way he has amassed more than a century of Test caps, fought off the xenophobia of small-minded politicians and, thanks to his extraordinary longevity in Super Rugby, had an entire Sharks campaign named after him. He has been in three Currie Cup-winning Sharks sides, two Super Rugby finals and a World Cup semi-final. In September 2019 he will embark on his third World Cup with the Springboks, hoping to go one better than the third-place finish at the 2015 tournament.

It must all seem a little surreal for the humble man from Harare, whose prodigious rugby talent sent him around the rugby-playing world, hearing his name roared by crowds from Auckland to London. In this book he speaks for himself, although you'll have to imagine the deep baritone speaking voice, a mixture of Johnny Cash and Paul Robeson. Where necessary I have added some explanation and quoted his family, friends and a clutch of great players who campaigned with and against him over the years.

In all my research and interviews one thing stands out above all else: no one has a bad word to say about Beast. He is universally respected as a rugby player and admired as a human being. I hope you enjoy his story.

Andy Capostagno
Lidgetton
September 2019

Chapter 1

BORN HUNGRY

My name is Tendai, which in the Shona language means 'Be thankful to God', but you can call me Beast. Apart from my family, everyone calls me Beast. I've been Beast since I was nine years old. I had a group of friends at primary school and the leader was a guy by the name of Kuda. He and I grew up in the same neighbourhood, playing soccer in the street, and we would see each other every day. He was my best friend and in the same class as me and I used to look up to him as a role model. One day he decided that I needed a nickname and everybody put their heads together. At one stage they called me 'Monster' and there were a few other names as well, but the one that stuck was 'Beast'. Wherever I play rugby, when I get the ball the crowd cries, 'Beeaasssttt!' so I guess I'm stuck with it!

My mum's name is Bertha and her family name is Kuhlengisa. My dad is Felix Mtawarira. My mum reminds me every second day what I was like as a child. I was a big baby. I weighed in at five kilos when I was born, which probably made me the biggest baby in Zimbabwe. So my mum had to endure the pain of that, and I was her first born, although I do have an older brother on my dad's side. She told me I had a huge appetite and as soon as they could, they had to supplement milk with solids.

My hunger grew and grew and when my younger brother Ray came along four years later, I used to eat his food as well. My mum is a great cook and she used to make a fantastic beef stew. When I go home to Zimbabwe now, that's the first thing she cooks for me. So my dad had to work hard just so they could feed me. He worked as a property manager for ZFC for 15 years and as a result of that he was able to give me the best start in life. We weren't rich and we weren't poor, we were in between. We had a roof over our heads and there was never a day in my life that I went without food.

My dad liked to remind me about Zimbabwe's fight for independence. They were recruiting young men to go fight in the uprising. He was a young adult at the time and his family didn't want him to get involved in the bush war, so they sent him away to study. I guess you could say he was a nerd! His family name was Mtawarira, but his clan name was Simbirori, which is the Shona name for a Fish Eagle. The Fish Eagle is a really strong bird, so when I was growing up I was reminded all the time that the Simbirori are strong; we don't back down from anything.

My dad was a good tennis player and also a Chelsea supporter, whereas I've always been a Manchester United fan, but I think my sporting genes come more from my mum's side of the family. She was a good netball player and her cousins were all good at sport. One of them was a particularly good rugby player who went to Peterhouse. My mum's genes have also helped my metabolism. I have been hungry my whole life, but no matter how much I ate it never turned to fat. I lived on huge amounts of sadza, or mealie pap, as it's known in South Africa. Sadza was what we ate every day at home. Maybe on Sunday we might eat rice, but that was all.

My dad expected a lot from us, and discipline was a big thing around the house. Unfortunately, I didn't like being disciplined and I was up and down all over the place. I used to give my mum headaches, and my dad thought I was going to be a rebel. I was strong and although they tried to discipline me I would fight the system.

My primary school was Prospect, which is in an area called Waterfalls in Harare. I was aggressive at Prospect, even with my mates. Not to put too fine a point on it, I was a bit of a bully and it's not something I'm proud of. Now I spend time in schools talking to kids about the negative effects of bullying; I guess I'm trying to make amends.

Kuda has always claimed that since he was the one who came up with my nickname, I should pay him royalties! He lives in Namibia now and works in marketing for one of the big companies there. We're still in touch and he got married last year. Tafadzwa was another of our group and he was quite smart, so we called him 'Brainiac' because he had the mind of a computer. He kind of disappeared off the radar after we left primary school, though.

I'm not sure where the name Beast came from, but we were all superhero fans, so maybe it came from The Beast in the X-Men. My favourite superhero was Captain Planet and I remember rushing home to catch his show on TV. Nowadays, of course, my favourite is Black Panther. I think black people have been misrepresented over the years in superhero movies and the reason Black Panther is so successful is that he represents excellence and so black people connect with him. Now I have a bit of a Black Panther connection, because the South African Super Rugby franchises campaigned under the Marvel banner in 2019 and the Sharks kit was based on Black Panther.

Once the boys dubbed me Beast it caught on quickly, probably because it suited my personality. Now, remember, at this time rugby wasn't yet part of my life. I was still playing soccer as a goalkeeper, but not a very good one. I used to try to spread myself as wide as possible and hope for the best, but I had a dream to play for Liverpool – Bruce Grobbelaar was their goalie at the time and he was my hero. But when I was nine or ten, Coach Walter arrived at school and his game was rugby. He started looking around for recruits to play rugby and he saw this big kid struggling to play in goal and decided that I needed to change codes.

I wasn't keen at first, but soon there was a group of us and we started learning the skills. We played barefoot and there was a kid called Tinashe Gorimani who was outstanding. He was big and fast and he scored tries like it was nothing and I remember being in awe of him. Coach Walter put me at flank, but I still wasn't enjoying the game.

I was a troublesome kid, but when I left Prospect Primary School I went to a really good high school and that's where I learned discipline and also where I fell in love with rugby. It was a boarding school, so I quickly had to conform and it wasn't easy.

I was 12 when I went to Churchill, quite a traditional school with lots of history behind it. It was renowned as a school that had a really good balance between sport and education.

Churchill produced soccer players such as Tinashe Nengomasha, who played for Kaizer Chiefs and is now at Wits, Willard Katsande (who was at Orlando Pirates and is now at Kaizer Chiefs), and of course Knowledge Musona, who plays in Belgium and is regarded as perhaps the best player ever to come out of Zimbabwe. In cricket there were lots of fine players, perhaps the best being Hamilton Masakadza, Tatenda Taibu and Stuart Matsikenyeri, who all played Test cricket. In fact Hamilton was still at Churchill when he scored a century on Test debut against the West Indies. At the time he was the youngest player in Test history to score a century in his debut game. In rugby, Churchill could claim Ray Mordt, the first Springbok to score a hat-trick against the All Blacks.

I was a boarder at Churchill, away from home for the first time, and the first problem was how to survive on the food they dished up there. They would feed us potatoes and rice, as well as sadza and lots of vegetables. My favourite was spinach and it still is, so maybe Popeye knew something. We didn't get meat every day, maybe five out of seven, so my dad kept me going by bringing me tuck every second week. He would bring lots of canned food, such as beans and fish, as well as dry foods like chips and nuts, because obviously I didn't have a fridge in my room. The school was okay with people bringing in extra food, but it was frowned on to eat in class. But I was always hungry, so I would always make sure I had my secret stash in my bag.

Churchill was renowned as probably the best rugby school in Zimbabwe, and it was there that the game became part of my life – where my passion grew. I borrowed my first pair of boots now and played on the flank at number seven. One of my schoolmates called Vandy played eight and he was really good, so we formed a formidable combination. We played together all the way through until, at Under-16, I was swapped to eight and it was then that I knew I was good at this game; I was running fast with the ball, enjoying the contact, enjoying every aspect of the game, and started to think I might be able to do something in rugby.

I was only 15 when I was drafted into the school's first team, but physically I was as big as or bigger than the rest of the side. At the time, I weighed 102 kilograms and stood about 1.79 metres tall. I remember a couple of games against our arch rivals, Prince Edward, who had a big Afrikaner kid by the name of Murray at number eight. He was built like a fridge and I remember going up against him as my opposite number and it was a big showdown. We managed to beat them in a tough contest; I scored a couple of tries and I remember relishing the challenge.

I loved being at Churchill, but I was obsessed with Peterhouse and the standards they had at the school, which were just incredible. I had three cousins there and the one I was closest to was Simba. I really envied him, and the interactions I had with the Peterhouse boys left a big imprint on me. I knew the school was out of my league and that there was no way my dad could afford to send me there, so the only way to get there was through my talents.

It was when Churchill played Peterhouse in Marondera that I really fell in love with the school. Just walking on the fields and hearing the way the kids talked was enough for me. It was a Saturday, Peterhouse had a very good Under-16 side and I was excited because this was my opportunity to impress the coaches, the rector, and whoever was watching. It was my chance to get a scholarship, I thought.

My cousin, Simba, was in their side and I went into full-on Beast mode. I played so well – I think I scored two tries – and later I heard boys talking about 'this kid, the Beast'. The Peterhouse coach was Paul Davies and after the game I plucked up my courage and went to speak to him. 'I want to come here and play for you,' I said. 'I promise I'll contribute and add value.' I gave him a whole long speech about what I would do for the school and at the end he said, 'As a rugby player you really do have something special. Unfortunately, Peterhouse doesn't give sports scholarships.'

I was broken, but he said he would raise the matter with the rector and that he would get a message to me through Simba. So a couple of weeks went by and I still hadn't heard anything, but I kept pestering Simba and eventually the news arrived; they don't do sports scholarships. No exceptions.

So that year I did my O Levels at Churchill and the next year started on my A Levels, but my dream never died. I knew I had to find a way, because I knew I belonged at Peterhouse. In the meantime, my studies had improved dramatically and my whole attitude had changed; I moved up from the fifth class to the first class, my grades went up and I went from being a young rebel, an angry child, to someone completely different.

It's no coincidence that at the same time that all of this was happening, I found the Lord. I remember being invited to a meeting at Churchill with some of my friends and was asked if I wanted to make a commitment. Until that moment I didn't really have a purpose in my life, but I made a decision and overnight my whole way of thinking changed. At the same time, my rugby improved and I realised that this was something I could pursue professionally. Everybody was telling me, you've got something special, take care of it, nurture it, work hard, and from the moment I found the Lord everything fell into place.

I had tried everything I could think of to get to Peterhouse. I even tried to arrange a payment plan with the school, but my dad just couldn't afford it. So it was that I stayed at Churchill, taking A Levels in Maths, Accounting and Business Studies, but somewhere deep inside I didn't feel complete. I made a decision; I said to myself, 'Tomorrow you're taking a bus and you're going to go and see the rector yourself and plead your case.'

I've always been strong willed. When I want something, I go for it with everything I have. I thought to myself, no one is going to fight for you, you have to fight for yourself. I didn't tell anyone at school or in my family; I didn't even tell Peterhouse I was coming. And so the next day, dressed in my Churchill uniform, I took a chicken bus and rode the 45-minute trip from Harare to Marondera. A chicken bus is one of those old buses where people either stand or sit on the floor and there are chickens and goats on board as well.

But when we got to Marondera the bus cruised straight past the entrance to Peterhouse, and I had to run forward to tell the driver that this was my stop. So I got off and walked back and, as I went through the school entrance, I thought, Wow, I'm here.' I was nervous, butterflies in the stomach, but it was about a 10-minute walk from the entrance to reception and, as I admired the setting and the playing fields, I began to calm down. The boarding houses were really imposing and everything I saw told me that this school stood for excellence.

When I got to reception there was a lovely lady waiting for me, Mrs Griggs, the school secretary. To this day I regard her as one of the best people I've ever met in my life. She looked at my Churchill blazer with a big smile on her face. She asked what I wanted and I said, 'I'm here to see the rector.'

'Do you have an appointment?' she asked.

'No, Ma'am.'

'What's it about?'

'I need to see him about coming here.'

'Okay, let me see if I can find him.'

She called his office but he was in a meeting, so she told me to sit down and wait, which is what I did for half an hour. While I waited I started to rehearse what I was going to say, because I knew that what I said in this meeting would either cause him to take it further or to say no straight away. Eventually, my time came and I went upstairs to the rector's office, sweaty and nervous. The rector was Jon Calderwood and he immediately put me at ease. 'How are you doing, Tendai? It's good to see you,' he said. 'How can I help you?'

So I said what I had rehearsed, that I really admired the school, felt I could add a lot of value, that I just wanted to come, contribute, give my life to the school. And then of course I had to confess that my family couldn't afford it, that I would need some kind of scholarship or aid from the school to realise my dream.

He told me, just as Paul Davies had, that the school didn't give sports scholarships. So I pleaded with him, said that my life would be incomplete if I didn't make it to Peterhouse – and that seemed to have some impact.

He said, 'So you took a bus to come here?'

'Yes, sir.'

'You didn't tell anyone?'

'No, sir.'

'You're missing class to be here?'

'Yes, sir.'

'It's amazing that you would do that, but the fact is we don't give sports scholarships. However, I'm going to take this to the Board of Governors. I don't want you to get your hopes up, but what I will do is arrange that you have lunch with the boys before you go.'

And that really hit home because, as usual, I was very hungry. So I left him and went to the dining hall and found some of my friends. There I was, in my Churchill blazer, and I felt simultaneously completely out of place and entirely at home, because the boys welcomed me straight away. I ate lunch and went for seconds and I remember enjoying the whole experience. I sat with my cousin, Simba, and he was just shocked. Aaron Denenga was also there; we had played against each other many times and he would go on to become one of my closest mates. Aaron said he and his friends would try to put pressure on the rector to help me out.

Eventually lunch had to end, of course, and I remember not wanting to leave. I just wanted to stay there, but I had to face reality and I had to get back to Churchill. The last thing I wanted was for my mum and dad to be angry with me for going missing, so I caught the chicken bus back, but this time there was a big smile on my face.

It was a week before the rector finally contacted me with the good news. He said that a few people in the meeting supported me because they knew about me and that I was a good guy. Paul Davies in particular spoke in my favour and eventually they agreed to let me come. But I could only enrol in January, at the start of the next academic year, so I had a long wait and subsequently I finished school a year later than I should have.

So now that the rector had said yes, I had to tell my parents. They couldn't believe it. My dad insisted that we couldn't afford it and I told him the only thing we had to pay for was my uniform. There was no anger, but they wanted to know all the details: How did I get there? What did I tell the rector? What would happen next? They were impressed and, at the end of the day, they appreciated the fact that I made it work, that I did it all myself. That's what amazed my dad the most.

So the next trip to Peterhouse was to the school shop to get the uniform – thankfully, they had some second-hand stuff that was much cheaper than buying new. But even so, I could only fit into the largest blazer they had and that had to last me for two years. The other day I was with my wife looking at old school photos and she asked, 'How did you move around?' The blazer was so tight it looked like the sleeves were about to burst at the seams, but that did nothing to diminish the honour I felt when I pulled it on for the first time.

Chapter 2

A PETERHOUSE BOY

Peterhouse is a group of schools that consists of Peterhouse Boys, Peterhouse Girls, Springvale House Preparatory School and Peterhouse Nursery School. The schools are situated in Marondera, some 72 kilometres east of Harare. Widely regarded as Zimbabwe's top independent boarding school and one of the premier independent schools in southern Africa, Peterhouse Boys was founded in 1955 and caters for approximately 500 boys from Form 1 to Form 6, all of whom are full-boarders.

Jon Calderwood, the rector who arranged for Beast to go to Peterhouse, had been part of the group of schools since the early1980s. He was the founding head of Springvale House, serving there for eight years from 1985, subsequently head of Peterhouse Girls until 2001 and he then served 11 years as the rector of Peterhouse Boys, before his retirement in 2012. Paul Davies, the rugby coach Beast tried to impress, is now retired and living in Fish Hoek in the Western Cape.

The day before my first day at Peterhouse I couldn't sleep I was so excited. The anticipation of what was coming grew as I put on my uniform: white shirt, blue tie, blue jacket – the number ones, as we used to call them – nice and formal. I felt like a man as I put on my superhero suit! I remember taking the drive with my mum on the first day; it took us about an hour to get there from Harare. So much was running through my head as we drove. I was visualising how I couldn't wait to play rugby for Peterhouse, how I couldn't wait to be part and parcel of daily life there, and you bet there were butterflies in my tummy.

There are six boarding houses at Peterhouse and I was assigned to Snell House. For some reason, Snell had a bad reputation; the boys who came out of there were the naughty ones, the ones who went against the grain. Obviously, they put me there to be a shining light and offer some positive energy! Anyway, I met the guys I was going to be boarding with and I was amazed at how spick and span everything was; I had never experienced anything like it before. There was a proper space to study, a place to put your bag, and cupboards. Cupboards may not seem like a big thing, but I was used to having a big trunk into which everything was packed and which was then stored under the bed. Now I had actual cupboards!

Everything was just over the top and it seemed to me that Peterhouse boys were spoilt – and that was fine by me. I wasn't about to let this opportunity go. I got really good grades in the O Levels I had sat at Churchill and now I was studying for three A Levels: Maths, Business Studies and Accounting. A very smart guy. It was something I grew up with. My dad always said, academics count number one in this house. He was always on my case, as well as that of my siblings.

Brian, my older half-brother, was the one who set the tone for our household both academically and athletically as per our father's household rules. Brian is three years older than me. We have always been close and he has set a great example for me. He was the first of the family to excel at school.

He played rugby in the centre for Old Hararians and he represented Zimbabwe at Under-21 level. He was very smart and I got a lot of direction from him, especially in terms of academics. By the time I started my A Levels, Brian was studying IT at Midlands State University in Gweru, between Harare and Bulawayo.

I immediately settled in at Peterhouse and was ready to tackle my studies. I met the staff, and my Maths teacher in particular had a big effect on me. We called him 'Pug' and he was always on my case.

He was surprised how a big guy like me could be good at Maths; his experience of rugby players was that they really weren't a good fit with Maths, but as it turned out I was second in class for the whole year – there was only one pupil at Peterhouse Girls who beat me. And the fact that my academics were so strong took a lot of the pressure off, because the last thing I wanted was for my dad to stop me from playing rugby.

Initially, of course, it was summer, so we did athletics instead of rugby and I also enjoyed playing basketball. I was a shot-putter and had been a hurdler at Under-16 level, but at Peterhouse I started competing in the 4x100 relay team. I was the starter because although it took me a while to get going, once I was into a rhythm I could really move! So I would give us a good start and hand the baton on to the guys in the middle, and then the anchor leg would be run by the best and quickest guy.

What was really happening was that I was doing speed work to improve my rugby. On the track I was doing 50-, 150- and 200-metre workouts and that really helped me be more explosive on the rugby field. There was no pushback from anyone. They could see how excited I was to be there and they were delighted just to have me on their side. Even the coach, Paul Davies, came to tell me how impressed he was with how I had made a plan to come to the school.

The rugby team had a number of really good players. Aaron Denenga on one wing, Taku Karimanzira – who we called 'Curry' – on the other. Aaron was a sprint champion and really fast, and in my second year he was switched to flank. Curry wasn't built like a wing, but he was deceptively quick and a great crash-ball runner. Then we had a good scrumhalf, Barry Mutsonziwa, small but with a big heart and, of course, Simba who played at lock but had explosive pace like a flank. Our flyhalf was something special; short and stocky, David Cloete could kick the ball a mile and he was signed up by the Sharks before I was. He was in his final year when I started at Peterhouse.

Paul Davies remembers Beast's effect on the team: 'He came into my side in the lower 6th [form], playing at number eight. He was extraordinarily strong and quick. He wasn't bulked up like he is now. We had a particularly good team, but Beast stood out. He was such a good player that he was unstoppable from a five-metre scrum. We devised a lot of strategies around him and frequently we used him as a decoy, because the opposition would put three players on him and that would open up the gaps elsewhere.'

While I was at school Zimbabwe was going through the whole land invasion thing and there was a serious brain drain at Peterhouse, with some teachers forced to leave the country. But there was never a chance that the school would close – simply because it was full of the children of ZANU-PF ministers. There were times when it was under pressure to change its name to something more politically correct, but that didn't happen.

Paul Davies remembers when the real world came to visit the school. 'The rector was arrested one day in 2004, along with the heads of a number of independent schools – men and women – and he spent two nights in prison in Marondera. He was very well known there and he said that when he walked into the cell, the only seat that was available was offered to him.

'The school is entirely fenced; we had an outside security company patrolling the grounds and we were never breached per se. One day we opened the gates and a group came in from the university. They were spoken to in the waiting room next to the rector's office. There was no violence, just a bit of noise and it was handled quite well because the police didn't want anything to occur. They kept a low-key presence outside. As is so often the case, the protestors were ill-informed. They didn't seem to realise that Peterhouse had lots of black pupils and had in fact been multi-racial for forever and a day. Obviously, however, if you could afford the fees to send your child to Peterhouse you weren't poor, so this was really about the haves and the have-nots.'

Important games were played on our main field – Field 11 – where the long-standing tradition was that only first-team players were allowed to walk across it; everyone else had to go around. My most memorable game in my first year at Peterhouse was against Falcon College, who were from Esigodini in Matabeleland. The pavilion and stands were filled with parents on one side and schoolboys on the other. As usual, I was wearing rugby boots borrowed from my friend, Gwinyai Murahwa. He had big feet like me, and I was so grateful he was happy to lend me his boots.

We ran out of the pavilion onto the field and the parents and kids formed a tunnel to let us through and sang the school war cry. We were so pumped up perhaps because everyone was convinced we were going to lose. They were the big, hardened farm boys and we were the city slickers.

The first thing I did was to make a big tackle on the Falcon fullback. He took a high ball and then tried to run around me, but he didn't make it and the crowd just went wild! But we fell behind early and Falcon were still five points ahead after an hour of play. So with less than 10 minutes left, I knew I had to do something. I used to love my eighth-man picks from the back of the scrum and this was a good time to do it because there was a big blindside. I picked up on the 22 and ran, beat the scrumhalf and the flanker, and scored in the corner. Now the scores were level and David Cloete banged over the conversion. From that point on we were never going to lose and it remains one of my fondest memories.

My first year at Peterhouse went by so quickly, but I enjoyed every moment. The rugby was great, but perhaps more importantly, I found a way to cure my hunger for food. I got to know the kitchen staff and they became my buddies, so every time there were leftovers they would give me a heads-up. Now I could get seconds and thirds whenever I wanted them and that was great because I had put myself on a protein diet to help with my gym regime. I needed to eat a lot, particularly off season, which was my time to pick up muscle.

I was very strong for my age and I particularly liked doing squats. I was bench pressing something like 205 kilograms at that point, so I needed a lot of food because I wasn't on supplements or anything drug related. It was purely food; I ate a lot and I turned it all into muscle. I used to do a lot of running. The first bad injury I got was when I was still playing Under-16, and it still bugs me today; I sprained both my ankles and I still have to strap them before every game. The only other bad injury was when I dislocated my thumb, but compared to everyone else, I got off lightly.

I built a good reputation during my first year, settling in quickly and making a positive impact, so I became a prefect and made deputy head of house at Snell. Traditionally, you couldn't captain the first team if you hadn't been at the school since Form 1, but they made an exception for me and I was made captain of the rugby team for my second year at Peterhouse.

Paul Davies made the decision and there weren't any arguments; as far as he was concerned, I was the best player and deserved the captaincy. He became a close friend and taught me a lot of life skills. In particular, he taught me to speak well because he was always on my case about grammar and would always remind me that a rugby player is a gentleman.

Paul remembers it well: 'He was an absolutely outstanding young man even then, but very quiet, rather like he is now. He gets

18

on with his life, but keeps a low profile. I made him captain and that caused a bit of a stir, because people said he hadn't been at the school long enough, but the rector backed the decision and that was that. He was the boys' choice as skipper as well, so there were no recriminations.'

My game took a step up because of my environment at Peterhouse. In my last year at Churchill I was selected to play for Zimbabwe Schools and in July 2002 we went to Pietermaritzburg for Craven Week. At that time I didn't know I was going to come to South Africa, but I knew I wanted to play professional rugby.

In my first year at Peterhouse I was once again picked for Zimbabwe Schools and this time Craven Week was to be played in Wellington in the Cape. I hadn't been approached by anyone in 2002, but this time Western Province made me an offer and someone from Tuks (University of Pretoria) also came to talk to me. The offers didn't really excite me because although some of my mates from the year before had done well – the Lions signed Brian Mujati and Aaron Denenga – the team I most enjoyed watching was the Sharks, and I certainly wasn't expecting anything from them. But fate was about to take a hand.

Beast wasn't eligible to play Craven Week in 2004 because he had already turned 19, but that year Peterhouse went on tour to KwaZulu-Natal. Paul Davies was in charge, and he made contact with an old friend. Tony Akal was the headmaster of St Henry's Marist College in Durban. He and Davies had worked together when Paul was headmaster of St David's Marist in Johannesburg. St Henry's was celebrating its 75th anniversary and to that end had organised a rugby festival. Paul Venter was the master in charge of

19

rugby at St Henry's and he recalls the day he discovered Peterhouse were coming: 'The first-team coach Mark Foster and I had organised the fixture lists and the invitations had been sent out. We invited Kingsway, St David's Marist, De La Salle and Marian College. Then the headmaster called us into his office and said, "I've invited Peterhouse." Mark looked at me and I said, "But they're a lot stronger than anyone else we've invited," but the deal had already been done.

'The financial realities of Zimbabwe at the time dictated that Peterhouse had to get the train from Harare, so it was my job to go fetch them. I got to the station and they got off the train, led by their captain, Beast. I took one look at him and got back on the bus to phone Mark. I said, "This fixture list, she's just been changed!"

'At the first game Peterhouse played it was immediately apparent that here was something special. The crowd picked up on his name quite quickly and you could hear people talking about this Beast fellow. I said to Mark, "We have to do something here," and I thought of Barry Angus. Barry had been the PE teacher at St Henry's until 1992 and now he was the conditioning coach at the Sharks. I phoned him and said, "You need to come and have a look at this."

'The next game Peterhouse played, Barry arrived with Garth Giles and they took one look and the rest was history. What struck me about him straight away was that, along with the sheer size of the boy, he was quite clearly an athlete, and after the first game you knew that he could seriously play the game. The problem with school rugby sometimes is that the really big kids can just run over players, *but Beast had the offload, he had searing pace and he had great hands.'*

Paul Davies remembers the day Beast's life changed: 'Everything was done very professionally, but in hindsight I should have told Beast that I was his agent, because Barry and Garth approached me after the game and asked for permission to speak to him! I said I would need to speak to Beast first, because by this time the touring side was around the swimming pool. I said, "These chaps want to interview you and I suggest you listen to them, but sign nothing until we get back to Zimbabwe."'

Barry Angus's connection to the school was the first thing that went Beast's way. The second was the involvement of Garth Giles. A former Natal scrumhalf and captain, Giles was intimately involved with every aspect of the feeder system into the Sharks. In particular, as director of coaching for the KwaZulu-Natal Rugby Union's junior sides, he was familiar with the best schoolboy talent in the province. He also had a soft spot for Peterhouse going back to his days as a schoolboy at Hilton College, when the two schools played against each other annually. And so, even though Peterhouse were too strong for their opponents, Giles could instantly assess the quality of Beast. Moreover, Giles had the respect of everyone involved at the Sharks Academy and his word was good enough to fling the gates of opportunity wide open.

Garth and Barry were impressed with my skill set and my pace, and after the game they came and met me and offered me a place at the Academy. They said they would organise a bursary for my studies and look after me and, well, you can just imagine the smile on my face. I could have burst with joy. I nearly made my Sharks debut that same Friday. They were looking for players for an Academy side to play Glenwood, and among their team was my friend David Cloete, the old Peterhouse flyhalf. But, in the end, sense prevailed and they said, let's do this properly.

So the tour ended, we went back to Zimbabwe, and I went home to tell my parents about the offer. I was so excited, but the first thing my dad said was: 'Are you sure you want to do this?'

I said, 'Am I *sure*? It's not even a question. This is what I want to do. It's what I've been waiting for.'

And he said, 'Those boys you're going to be playing against are big. They'll probably hurt you.'

Well, that made me mad. I couldn't believe my dad would actually say something like that. I didn't express my anger at the time, but I said to myself, 'Okay, I'm gonna show you.' I took it as a challenge. Looking back now, I realise that sport wasn't really my dad's thing and when I came back from South Africa and told him that this is what's happening, he couldn't quite swallow it. His idea was for me to finish school, go to college, and get a job, so maybe what he was doing was throwing a curve-ball, just to see how serious I was.

Back in the real world, it was time for me to sit my A Levels. I creamed my Maths and got an A+, got a C in Accounting and we won't talk about my Business Studies … My place at the Academy was confirmed and, with my exams out of the way, it was a case of trying to stay fit before leaving. My dad had been posted to Bulawayo, so that's where we were when school finished and I went into a training regime on my own, walking 10 kilometres to the gym and back every day. Then a family I knew from church was kind enough to donate a bike so I didn't have to walk. It meant a lot to me; I was a man on a mission.

It worked out perfectly because Bulawayo is the opposite of Harare. There aren't too many distractions, if you know what I mean. Dead quiet. A ghost town. So much so that my brother and I used to go running on the tar road and were able to kick up-and-unders to each other. We would run round the neighbourhood and force cars to stop while we completed a catch under a high ball.

I also used to train with Mandla Gijima, who was at Christian Brothers' College Bulawayo. He was a really good athlete, doing the 200- and 100-metre sprints, and became Zimbabwe's champion. He was a freak, as quick as Tonderai Chavhanga, and he was awarded a sports scholarship to America. I owe Mandla a lot because he helped me with my speed and agility work. We trained together on the road and in the gym for about a month and I got so much better. So by the time I got to the Academy I was fit and quick and strong.

Looking back on my time training with Mandla, I realise now that I missed out on a few normal teenage things. The Leavers Ball at Peterhouse; the big parties thrown by my mates; I wasn't even thinking about them. All I was thinking about was getting myself in the best possible shape and condition for the Sharks Academy. I was zoned in. Mandla was about to take up his scholarship and so, during that time, we became really close and would confide in each other. If I was feeling nervous or uneasy about what was coming I could open up to him and chat, and it worked both ways, and he would share his fears about going to America. I think, though, that basically we were both excited about the future.

Sadly, it didn't work out for Mandla in America. He was one of the most talented athletes to come out of Zimbabwe, and he got himself into the best shape possible, but when he got there he got the shock of his life. He found out he was way behind and not as strong as he should have been according to American stand-ards. He had to put on a lot of weight, about 10 kilograms of muscle, and the next thing he started struggling with hamstring tears and injury after injury.

So his athletics career didn't really take off, but he finished his studies and stayed over there for about seven years. Now he is back home where he runs an athletics academy that helps identify talent in the schools in Bulawayo. I met up with him there recently and it was a really emotional reunion. We hadn't seen each other in about 12 years and it brought it all back; how hard we had worked together and how much he pushed me.

Chapter 3

SWIMMING WITH SHARKS

Anyway, back in 2004, it was time for me to leave home and go live in South Africa. I had another pep talk from my dad, telling me not to be distracted and stuff like that, and some of it registered, but a lot went over my head because I was just in my zone. My mum was always the pillar of strength in our family and she prayed for me and for everything to go well. I had always looked up to my mum because she taught me from a young age that our strength comes from God.

I was due to report to the Sharks Academy on January 6th, 2005, but I took the Greyhound from Bulawayo on December 26th – Boxing Day – because there were a few things that had to be sorted out. I travelled light; in my tog bag I had my Mitre boots (the ones donated to me when I was still at school), a couple of T-shirts and a few pairs of shorts – no warm clothes – and R2000 from my dad. I also had a study visa organised by the Academy and my most prized possession, my Discman, which was what we listened to before MP3s and iPods.

I couldn't go anywhere without my music. I loved hip hop, R&B and gospel, so my CDs kept me company during the six hours it took to get to Beit Bridge, the border post between Zimbabwe and South Africa. It took about two hours to get across and our first stop in South Africa was in Musina, the closest big town. There are lots of Zimbabweans in Musina and it was my first chance to spend South African rands instead of Zimbabwean dollars.

I didn't sleep much on the journey; I just listened to my music and daydreamed about what the Academy would be like. But I was seated next to a girl and we got talking. Turned out she was on her way to study at Rhodes University and she asked me why I wasn't sleeping. I told her I was too excited about going to the Academy and she thought that was cool and we chatted for a couple of hours. We got off the bus in Johannesburg, and she boarded one that was going to Grahamstown – now Makhanda – but we exchanged numbers and actually became good friends.

Eventually, I caught the bus to Durban, arriving on the morning of December 28th. There to meet me was the manager of Durban High School Old Boys, the club I had been placed with by the Academy. He took me to the rugby house and I got to meet my roommates, most of whom were from the Eastern Cape, among them Ian Ndlovu, Vukile Vusi and S'bu Ndungane, the younger brother of the twins Akona and Odwa who both played for the Springboks.

None of us knew much about Durban, so in the first few days we took a taxi to the city to see what it was like, and also went to Kings Park Stadium to look at the facilities and to take in the atmosphere on the outer fields. When I had come with Peterhouse we were based in Glenwood and hadn't had the chance to get to Kings Park. There was nobody there at that time of year, but it was still special and I thought, 'This is it, this is what I'm here for.'

There was a problem, however. I was hungry – again! I thought that being part of the rugby house at DHS Old Boys, my meals would be taken care of, but they weren't. We were left to fend for ourselves and all I had was the R2 000 my dad had given me. Now I had to study and train and catch taxis, so although I was grateful to have a room in the house, I was a little disappointed. One thing that kept me going was KFC. There was no KFC in Zimbabwe and when I heard that there was chicken that was both cheap and so good it became my go-to meal. I would eat about 10 'Streetwise Meals' at a time and for a while I had KFC every single day. I was 19, so my body could process it, but I wouldn't recommend it.

It became apparent, though, that I could not carry on this way. Things improved when I heard about a church in Hillcrest that was run by people I knew from back home. They heard my story and immediately took me under their wing. Home-cooked meals were now a thing. They also introduced me to Graham Mackenzie, president of College Rovers Rugby Club. Graham had heard of me and straight away offered to help – but there was a problem.

I had signed an agreement with DHS Old Boys and had already started pre-season training with them. The people in charge saw how fit and strong I was and were very excited about me playing for them, so when I told them I wanted to move to College Rovers they tried everything they could to keep me. The matter ended up going through an arbitration process at the Academy and thankfully everyone saw sense. They wanted me to stay for selfish reasons, of course, but the Academy basically said, 'If the kid doesn't want to play for you, what's the point? Why stand in his way? Let him enjoy himself.'

So I was able to move from where I was staying in Durban North to Morningside, which is much closer to Kings Park. I didn't have to catch a taxi any more either, because I could walk straight across. Life became a lot easier, and a lady by the name of Bridget became my best friend. She was attached to College Rovers and she would prepare meals for me every day and drop them off at the Academy. If she was going away, she would leave two to three days' worth of food for me. An Angel.

Once the Academy started, I got a good lunch every day and also met guys such as Keegan Daniel and Craig Burden who were in their second year. Then Ryan Kankowski returned from playing Sevens with the Blitzbokke. Also at the Academy then were guys like JP Pietersen, Brad Barritt and Waylon Murray.

I started playing for College Rovers Under-20s at blindside flank, with Craig Burden at openside and Ryan Kankowski playing eight when he wasn't playing for the Blitzbokke. Our coach was Kevin Stevenson and he decided that, when Ryan was available, he would move me to lock. Can you believe that? Of course, I basically played like a loose forward and I didn't jump in the lineouts. Anyway, despite having to accommodate a non-jumping lock, we had a really good season and won the league.

I was hungry for success – and also hungry for food. The restaurant Circus Circus at the Suncoast Casino on the Durban beachfront had a special every Thursday: a kilo of steak, 500 grams of chips and a litre of cool drink. If you could finish that in 30 minutes they would give it to you for free. Well, the first time I did it, I finished in 12 minutes. A new record! They couldn't believe it; they actually searched me to see if I was hiding some of the chips, but that was me. No indigestion, no problem. I went back a few more times and then they started adding ice cream to the challenge to make it more difficult, but I still finished in time.

As far as I was concerned, it was free food and I was poor, so every Thursday Craig Burden would pick me up and we'd go to Circus Circus. Sometimes Craig wouldn't eat anything himself, but just watch me, and we did that for a whole year. Eventually the management said, sorry, but this is too much now, and I was banned. 'No problem,' said Craig, 'there's another Circus Circus in town and they have the same special. We'll go there.' But when we got there, there was a picture of me on the wall, saying this man is not allowed to take the challenge!

When the time came for the Sharks to announce their squad for the Under-21 campaign, I wasn't in it. Swys de Bruin was the coach and although he knew about me, I wasn't selected. Instead of feeling down about it, I realised that what I needed to do was to work even harder and, as luck would have it, at the first training session one of the guys was injured and I was called up.

At my first session, Sangoni 'Mox' Mxoli was there. During my time at the Academy, Mox was the biggest name. He had played loosehead prop for SA Schools two years in a row and was a physical freak. In the gym he could do squats while holding

65-kilogram weights – even the senior guys couldn't do that. People would go to the gym just to watch him. I was also strong in the gym, but not like Mox, and he was clearly earmarked to go straight into the Currie Cup team.

Although I was now with the training squad, nothing was guaranteed. I made sure I worked as hard as I possibly could to impress Swys. The first Under-21 game of the season was against the Lions – on paper, they were the strongest side and had some big names, such as Jean Deysel and Rory Kockott. And this time around, when Swys announced the Sharks side I was in ... at lock. Swys said to me, 'I know you're a flank, but remember that the number on your jersey doesn't determine the way you play.' Swys's big thing was, go out there and express yourself; he's still like that today.

So we played on the Crusaders field next to Kings Park and here I was running around with the number four on my back. Nikolai Blignaut was my lock partner and it looked hilarious, because he was a foot taller than me. I wasn't the only one playing out of position; Kanko (Ryan Kankowski) was moved from eight to 13, with Burden playing flank and wing in the same game. The Lions were the defending Under-21 champions and no one gave us a chance, but we ended up outplaying them. I guess it proved that the coach knew what he was doing, so I played the whole season for the Sharks at lock. We didn't win the tournament, but we beat lots of good sides, including Western Province in Cape Town.

Up until that point I was being looked after by College Rovers, who paid me R300 a week pocket money. For that I was expected to clean or tend bar at the club. That money went a long way; I bought myself new boots and the odd treat. But at the end of the season the Sharks approached me and offered me a junior contract and I was finally able to earn some proper money. They paid me R2000 a month and because it was a two-year contract, for the first time I had some security. It might not seem like a lot today, but believe me, at the time, I was the man. I could buy as much KFC as I wanted.

Just like the kid in Bulawayo missing out on high school life, very little had changed when I was in Durban. Guys would come around and invite me out to party, binge and to meet and hang out with girls. But none of that remotely excited me. I think some of them even worried about me and most of them thought I wasn't normal. To be honest, for a kid my age, I wasn't. I was focused; you might actually say I was too focused. Rugby was my only interest. During weekends (and Christmas), I spent time with the family I knew from church in Hillcrest. I was being looked after, so my parents never worried.

In January 2006 the Academy resumed and I returned to my studies. My BComm was going well. The club season was set to start in March, so I had two months to prepare for that. One day I went to see the coach, Kevin Stevenson, and made him aware of my intention to play flank. So I began the season at flank, but as soon as Kanko came back from Sevens I was pushed back to lock again.

I was frustrated, but around that time I landed a job working as a bouncer at One Stop, the nightclub in the hospitality section at Kings Park. I knew Chris, the owner of the club, through College Rovers, because he was the landlord for the accommodation I stayed in. So I would play for the Sharks Under-21s on a Saturday and then stay at One Stop as a bouncer until about 1am. The head bouncer was a guy called Tony and he used to look after me. He knew I was just a rugby player trying to earn some bucks and when fights started he would keep me away from them. So I never had to deal with the ugly side and the worst it got for me was to help some drunk guy out of the club.

I was paid R300 for a Saturday night and with that, together with my Sharks contract, I could now budget properly for myself, buy some clothes and other stuff. I was usually in bed by 2am and up for church on Sunday morning at 9am. Sleep has always been very important to me – second to food, of course.

The season continued with the Sharks Under-21s and I was still at lock, but playing like a flank. I was running around, making tackles, fielding high balls, but unbeknownst to me, Swys had been chatting to Dick Muir, coach of the Sharks Super Rugby team. The two of them apparently agreed that I had a lot of talent, but they couldn't decide which position I could play for the Sharks in senior rugby.

Chapter 4

BACK TO FRONT

In June 2006 I got a call from Dick Muir asking if I would come see him in his office the next day, and the first thing that went through my mind was that he wanted me for the Sharks Currie Cup team. I was so excited I couldn't sleep and when I got to his office he made me feel comfortable straight away. I had been at the Academy for 18 months, but this was the first time I had got to meet Dick face to face. He smiled, cracked a few jokes, called me his Zimbabwean brother and before I knew it I was relaxed.

Then he floored me: 'Beast, I really like you and I think you're a great player, but the fact of the matter is, I don't think you can make it at flank. Maybe you would make it at provincial level in that position, but you'll never be a Springbok, and I want to make you a Springbok!'

Dick remembers the encounter well: 'I just remember seeing this unbelievable athlete. He was incredibly strong and athletic, but not tall enough to be a lock, maybe not quick enough to be a flank at the top level, but with his power, what I saw there was an opportunity to move him to the front row. It took a little bit of persuasion. He originally didn't quite buy into it, but once he did he never looked back and he's been a stalwart for the Sharks.

'He had help from Balie Swart, but he had good guys around him, like Jannie and Bismarck du Plessis, Deon Carstens and BJ Botha. They were all really good players and they stood by him through the tough times. It was a time in the Sharks' history where there was a lack of really good players and we had to go out and find players who could be potential Springboks.

'I remember saying to Beast at the time, "You'll play for the Sharks at lock or flank, but you won't play 100 games and you won't play for the Springboks in those positions." It was an easy decision to say to Beast, "If you convert to prop you'll play 100 games and you'll become a Springbok great." He did it and hats off to him on what he's been able to achieve with an immense amount of hard work.

'Now that he's been around for so long you see the effect he has on the dressing room. When he pulls on the jersey, the other players say, "Wow, we've got this guy on our side today! Thank goodness." He's a leader within our organisation and he's a leader amongst the Springboks and to have him is just phenomenal.'

At the time, however, Beast thought the bottom had fallen out of his world.

All the time Dick's talking about the Springboks, the only thing I'm thinking is that I want to be a Shark. So Dick goes on and he says, 'You've got the physique of a loosehead prop,' and at that point my heart began to sink and I felt as if the ground beneath my feet was about to swallow me whole. He said, 'I think if you switch to loosehead you can be really successful.'

I sat down and gulped – this was really not what I expected. I was in total shock. Dick went on, 'I'll get the best people to help you and you'll have extra hours set aside to work with them and I guarantee you now, in fact I'll make you a promise, that if you make this work, you've got a spot in my team. That's all I wanted to say, so take some time to take it in and then come back to me when you're ready. This is what I see as your path going forward, so let's make it work.'

When I left his office I was distraught and I went to the nearest bathroom, sat down and cried my eyes out. My emotions overcame me; I was weeping and saying to myself, 'This is not what I've been working so hard for, what I've sacrificed so much for. I want to play in my position. If I change it's probably going to take me years to get it right.' That's the way I saw it; a long-term thing. Then I prayed to the Lord for guidance and understanding and eventually I pulled myself together.

Back at the Academy house, my eyes were so red that the boys could see straight away that there was something wrong. Someone said, 'You look down. Somebody die?' So I told them that I'd been to see Dick and he had told me he wanted me to play prop and they all went, 'Whoa!'

But while everybody else was sympathising and feeling sorry for me, there was a young flank by the name of Thabo Mamojele who saw what no one else saw – an opportunity! I remember him saying to me, 'You know what, Beast, this could actually be exactly what you have been working so hard for all this time. Maybe this is your big opportunity.' It was in that moment that my whole mindset changed; it was almost like a God-sent message. Thabo's words held so much weight because he was just a guy like me, a player, a youngster. He was talking to me from a mate's point of view and that struck a chord in me that prompted me to make the call. I immediately picked up the phone to Dick. 'Coach, I'm 110% in,' I said, 'I'm going to make this happen.'

Dick was very pleased and he told me that Balie Swart would be the man who would guide me through the transition. That was on the Friday and when I walked into Balie's office on the Monday, he told me he'd spoken to Dick and his first instruction was, 'Get yourself a notebook and keep it with you all the time.' So that's what I did; we would walk around together and Balie would give me pointers wherever we were – on the field, in his office – just as ideas occurred to him about the basics of prop-forward play. Where to hold my arm; techniques of scrumming; things I had to work on.

One thing we didn't have to work on was my body. I was already strong and doing the right stuff in the gym; I weighed 110 kilograms, which is the ideal weight for a loosehead, so the only thing I had to work on was technique. On the field we would put the ideas in my notebook into practice; we did some core and elastic exercises and then, of course, there was the scrum machine. I remember the first time I hit a scrum machine I wondered what on earth was going on. My body felt like it was in a really unnatural position and my neck and shoulders hurt and I wondered how I was supposed to get used to this.

But I learned to brush those negative thoughts away. I kept saying to myself, keep at it, keep at it, keep at it. After many hours of work with Balie, he said, 'It's time to put you under another player's wing.' That's how I came to meet BJ Botha, who was the first-choice tighthead with the Sharks at the time. BJ took on the role of father figure and he would call me 'Son'. He would say stuff like, 'Come here, Son, let me teach you a thing or two.' And he would pin me in awkward positions and my neck would be so sore the next day that I couldn't move it.

Those were tough times. I was hurting in places I never knew existed! There were many nights when I lay alone, feeling the aches and strains; nights when I wondered whether I had made a huge mistake. But my mentors helped me through it and BJ, in particular, taught me the basics: get your arm up, look where your elbow is, keep it straight, get your arse out and your back parallel to the ground. It took a few weeks of unbelievable pain, but from there I just started getting better and better and, after missing a few games for the Under-21s, it was decided that I was ready to have a go at prop in a club game.

Dick sent me down to Rovers to play for the third team, on the understanding that if it went well I would play for the Sharks in the Currie Cup against Griquas the following week. But when I got to the ground and walked onto the field I couldn't do it; I chickened out! I just said to myself, no, I'm not doing this, and slunk back to the rugby house with my tail between my legs. The fear hit me; what if this doesn't work out?

On the Monday, Dick called me into his office and asked me how it went. 'Fine,' I replied. 'It went well.' So Dick, satisfied with my answer, told me to get ready as he was going to play me this weekend, but from the bench. I was so naïve; I just thought, 'I hope he doesn't find out.' But the rugby world is small and, so Dick called Sean Everitt, who was the Rovers coach, to find out how I played. And it fell to Sean to tell Dick that Beast hadn't pitched!

I was in big trouble ... My phone rang, and it was Dick. 'Beastie, you need to come to my office and explain something.' It was Tuesday morning and I knew he knew. Dick said, 'Beastie, I have one rule. One thing I don't accept is lying.' And so I broke down and told him what had happened, how when the time came I had panicked, and he said, 'That's fine, being scared is okay, but don't ever lie to me again. Plans for this weekend have changed. You need to go play a few club games. One is not going to be enough.'

My heart sank – my dream of playing in the Sharks jersey had vanished. At the back of my mind, I had thought that Monday's meeting with Dick proved that he was prepared to back me and, because of that, I wanted that jersey now, not in a few weeks' time ... now. But I was grateful to be given a second chance and so that weekend I finally started a game with a number one on my back.

Things were going well; I got through the first couple of scrums and had just started to settle. Then, in the twentieth minute, I went to pick up the ball for a drive and got hit hard from the side. My knee gave way and I couldn't carry on. They got me off the field and it turned out to be an MC (medial collateral ligament) injury and that was me out for six to ten weeks.

Initially, there was nothing I could do, training wise, so I went back to school with Balie and we watched videos together. We watched a lot of Deon Carstens, who was the Sharks' first-choice loosehead at the time. Deon was a dynamic player who carried the ball in the loose and I enjoyed that aspect, but really I was focusing on what he was doing at set-piece time. For me these sessions were like muscle memory and slowly I started to recover and could get back in the gym. I did a lot of upper-body work and started to strengthen my core muscles, which are the most important ones for a prop. Eventually I came back to fitness and played a few minutes for Rovers off the bench. It went okay and so for the last couple of games in the Under-21 Currie Cup, Dick decided to put me on the bench. The first game was in Johannesburg against the Lions and then we played the Bulls. Mox Mxoli was the starting loosehead and I replaced him for the last 20 minutes in each game.

Dick could see a vast improvement and when it came time to announce the training squad for the 2007 Super Rugby season, my name was in there! We trained in November and December and then had two weeks off for Christmas. I was really excited because I was strong and fit and this was where I wanted to be, ready to take my chance.

That year Dick came with something new for training: boxing and wrestling. I had never done those sports before, but I turned out to be a natural at wrestling and the other guys would step out of the ring when they'd had enough of me. We would go to a dojo just a few hundred metres from Kings Park and it could get up to 40 degrees inside in the height of summer. We would grapple and box and it was torturous. In all the pre-season training I've had since then nothing compares. I enjoyed it and Bizzy – Bismarck du Plessis – was a good wrestler, but the senior guys hated it; they couldn't wait for it to end, but it lasted three months, with just the

Christmas break for rest.

The on-field training continued alongside and there was a lot of running and, for me, a lot of scrumming. This was my chance to work with Balie in a live situation, up against BJ Botha, John Smit, Deon Carstens and Bizzy, so my technique really improved because those guys made it tough for me. Balie taught me so much, but in the end he said I had to focus on three things: a straight back was the number-one priority – 'the coffee table', he used to call it, 'so I can have my meal there'; left arm up was number two; and number three was feet under the hips. With those three thoughts, the rest became muscle memory, working with my head up on the engagement, stuff like that.

So when the season began and I had to face other tightheads, I was ready, purely because of the intensity we brought to pre-season training. Remember that BJ Botha was the starting Springbok in that position at the time and he would drill me in training, to the extent that all parts of my body hurt after a session. I actually think that because of the quality of the people I was training with I grew more – and faster – than I would have been able to do in match situations.

Obviously, Dick had been watching me and he sat me down one day and told me about the long-term plan: that I probably wouldn't play for the Sharks that season, a couple of games at the end of the year at most, and then he would start to ease me in gradually the following year. And I nodded my head, but inside I was thinking, 'Not a chance. I want to play now. I'm not sitting on the sidelines, I'm ready.'

The first time I had a chance to try out what I had learned

was in a warm-up game against the Cheetahs at Kings Park in January of 2007. I packed down against CJ van der Linde, who was the other Springbok tighthead alongside BJ. Deon Carstens started the game for us and I came off the bench and I remember being so hyped up that I could have exploded.

So the first scrum came and it was just perfect; my body position was right, we got the perfect hit, and from there everything just came naturally. I remember pushing off CJ on his own ball and the expression on his face was like, 'What's this?' I was excited and just wanted to show Dick that I was ready. And he obviously felt the same way, that things were really working out.

The Sharks had a great draw for the Super 14 in 2007, with six home games in the first two months. Their first away match was against the Cheetahs in Bloemfontein in Week 6. The season began with a match against the Bulls at Kings Park on February 3rd. Deon Carstens was the starting loosehead, with Gideon 'Kees' Lensing on the bench. Lensing was a Namibian who had played for his country in the 2003 World Cup. He had a few good seasons for the Bulls, then spent the 2005/6 season with Leeds in England. When he came back to South Africa, Dick Muir signed Lensing as cover for the 2006 Currie Cup season. In the game against the Bulls, BJ Botha picked up an injury, so Carstens moved to tighthead for the second match and Lensing started at loosehead, which opened up a spot on the bench.

I was sitting back thinking, 'There's no way he's going to use me,' but on Tuesday evening when the team to play the Waratahs was announced, my name was among them. I was shocked. I

41

couldn't sleep the whole week. It was surreal. Even though I had worked so hard for it, given it everything, sacrificed so much – even giving up on going home for the holidays – still I couldn't believe it. Being named on the bench was the best moment of my life.

The Waratahs tighthead was Al Baxter, who had been the first choice in his position for the Wallabies. I spent the next four days studying him, and when match day arrived the weather was bright and clear. The Sharks made a slow start and Percy Montgomery exchanged penalties with Peter Hewat. The big moment came with about 20 minutes left in the game. There was a scrum and it was at that moment Dick decided to make the change, so I leapt off the bench and raced onto the field. I had this thing I used to do when I was really excited – I used to growl like a lion – and when John Smit heard me he had to tell me to calm down!

When we engaged at the scrum it was just like it had happened in the warm-up game with the Cheetahs. Everything went perfectly; I was as solid as a rock and we got really good ball from the scrum. I hadn't been on the field long when Butch James scored a try and that proved to be the decisive moment. I nearly scored from a drive close to the line, but I was held up – and that's the story of my life. I have been held up so many times it feels like somebody's out to get me!

In retrospect, probably the most significant thing to happen in that game wasn't on the field, but in the stands. I was still part of the Sharks Academy and at home games all the Academy guys sit in the main stand above the dugout, close to the tunnel where the players run out. That day they were there as usual and the first time I got the ball, one of the students shouted out, *'Beeaassstttt!'*

And the next time I got the ball the other Academy guys joined in and the crowd picked up on it. Before I knew it the whole stadium was screaming *'Beeaassstttt!'* and it moved from stadium to stadium as the season progressed. Bizzy was the first to make a fuss of me at training and would growl 'Beeaassttt!' whenever I got the ball. Craig Burden and Keegan Daniel were the next to latch on to the idea, and before you knew it, everyone was doing it. But it all started with a bunch of my Academy mates against the Waratahs.

Chapter 5

SO NEAR AND YET SO FAR

The Sharks beat the Waratahs 22–9, having prevailed 17–3 in the opening match against the Bulls. BJ Botha recovered to take his place at tighthead for the 23–16 win against the Highlanders at Kings Park the following week. Beast dropped out of the match-day squad, but then Muir was forced to make some key changes. Botha was again unfit for the Crusaders game and Carstens started in the number-three jersey. Lensing was omitted from the squad and did not feature again in the 2007 season, replaced by a youngster by the name of Pat Cilliers. Coincidentally, the day of the game was Cilliers's twentieth birthday and the former Michaelhouse pupil had a ringside seat for what turned out to be the match of the season. He remained in that seat, however, with Muir deciding not to risk him as the match raced to an incredible conclusion. What that meant was that Tendai 'Beast' Mtawarira, in his starting debut for the Sharks, played all 83 minutes.

I didn't think Dick was going to start me. I really thought he would go with Kees's experience, especially since I hadn't been in the squad the previous game. But at training on the Tuesday he came up to me and said, 'You're starting, Beastie. You ready?' I sure was. I showed some emotion during the game and it was against the Crusaders that I earned my first ever turnover scrum. Their tighthead was Campbell Johnstone, who had played three Tests for the All Blacks in 2005. He was a tough guy, a seasoned campaigner still in his prime and he taught me a couple of lessons. My neck got twisted in ways it hadn't before, but now he wasn't just scrumming against one guy who happened to be realising his childhood dream, he was scrumming against a whole stadium screaming, *'Beeaasssttt!'*

The match against the Crusaders was a defining one for the Sharks in 2007. The Canterbury-based franchise won the Super Rugby title seven times in 11 seasons from 1998, including in both 2005 and 2006. They were top-heavy with All Black superstars, including Richie McCaw, Dan Carter and Kieran Read. Significantly, however, 2007 was a World Cup year and the New Zealand Rugby Union withdrew key players from the first half of Super Rugby. Both McCaw and Carter stayed at home in New Zealand when the Crusaders went on tour to South Africa.

Nevertheless, the defending champions had hammered the Cheetahs 49–28 in Bloemfontein before travelling to Durban to play the Sharks and started the game as favourites. A fast-paced contest saw the Sharks score tries through Albert van den Berg and Bismarck du Plessis, but the Crusaders replied with two of their own from Read and Mose Tuiali'i. When the 80-minute hooter sounded the Crusaders led 26–20 and actually had a chance to kick the ball dead to close out the game. Instead they sent it deep into Sharks territory and the home side kept the ball through a number of phases before launching one final attack.

Sharks and Springbok wing Odwa Ndungane remembers the game: 'We had a nice, planned play that we had practised in the week. AJ Venter at eight would pick up the ball from the scrum and run wide, then give a back flip to flanker Jacques Botes. Jacques would draw the fullback and give the ball to me running the support line. So it duly happened that we got a scrum 15 metres from the Crusaders line and everything worked perfectly. AJ drew the flank away from the scrum with his wide run, back-flipped to Jacques, who now had only one man to beat, and he then gave me the ball with the try line in front of me. And I dropped the ball over the line!

'In my defence, it was really hot and humid and the ball was slippery, but even so … Anyway, time was running out and we were a few points behind and that knock-on was playing over and over in my head. With seconds left in the match, we turned the ball over to the Crusaders and they could have just kicked it into the stands, but they chose to play. As luck would have it, we got the ball back – either AJ or Deon Carstens got it back for us, I think. I was on the right wing and the ball was going left and for some reason I knew I had to be as close to the ball as possible.

'Adi Jacobs made a great break and I sprinted to keep up with him. He gave me the ball and I now had the fullback to beat. I had to make a split-second decision whether to look for someone else to pass the ball to or go for the corner. I decided to go for it and the fullback, Scott Hamilton, got his hands to me, so there was a bit of suspense because the TMO had to decide whether one of my feet *had touched the touchline. It was given and now Ruan Pienaar had to convert to win the game. He had kicked well all season and, as I watched the ball sail over the crossbar, it was one of the greatest feelings of my career. Of course, with the benefit of hindsight, it also meant that we qualified for a home final.'*

Beast remembers the celebrations as the scoreboard registered Sharks 27, Crusaders 26:

We picked up Ruan and Adi and carried them around the ground. It was such an important moment for us. We were a happy team and we did a lot of things together. John Smit and AJ Venter were the leaders in the squad and there were some incredible individuals amongst us. Ruan was one of the finest players I ever saw; he wasn't particularly big or strong, but he could do freakish things on the field. Butch James was always the man who got us laughing. We enjoyed each other's company, but that didn't stop us from training hard and when we got on the field we did what was expected of us.

Dick was important to the whole dynamic. He understood that if we were happy off the field we would deliver on it and to that end the discipline was left in the hands of the senior players in the squad. Dick knew how to press the right buttons in players and he could bring out the best in people. As soon as he had made the decision to make me a part of the match-day squad things changed dramatically for me. For one thing, I got my first sponsored car.

I used to ride my bike from my flat to training at the stadium. It was a bit of a secret that I didn't want anybody to find out about and all was fine until I started playing Super Rugby. The first thing that happened was that my monthly salary increased sixfold, so I was able to spoil myself with some luxuries, such as new shoes. I was also able to send more money home to my parents via Western Union, but I was still cycling to work and when Dick found out he went crazy! 'He doesn't have a car! Why didn't I know about this sooner? He's a precious commodity, I can't have him cycling back and forth.'

Butch James, the Sharks flyhalf at the time, remembers Beast's method of transportation: 'Beast's bike was something that everyone knew about. Whether he was coming to training or physio, whatever. He is quite a sweaty oke anyway, but being in Durban where it's hot and humid exacerbated the situation.'

So calls were made and a sponsored car was arranged, but what Dick didn't know was that I didn't have a driver's licence. I had to set up some lessons pronto and it was neck and neck that the car arrived at the same time as the licence. John Smit used to tease me about it, but through the grace of God I passed my test first time and the car arrived about halfway through the season. It was a little overwhelming, though, to go from a bike to a huge 4x4, and parking was a very daunting experience. I used to make sure I got to Kings Park early and would find the biggest space possible so that I didn't have to reverse.

John Smit remembers the transition from bike to car very well. He says, 'He rode his bike everywhere and then out of nowhere this sponsored car appeared and the Sharks players all learned quickly to park 300 metres away from Beast in order to protect their cars.'

By the time the Brumbies came to Kings Park at the end of March, the Sharks had won six out of six in Super Rugby and were top of the log. Those six wins included three against New Zealand opposition; the Crusaders (27–26), the Highlanders (23–16) and the Hurricanes (27–14). But the next fortnight brought a reality check as the Sharks lost twice to Australian teams, 10–21 to the Brumbies in Durban and 12–22 to the Force in Perth. A record win (59–16) against the Reds in Brisbane got the season back on track, but Beast's delight was tempered by what happened at the airport the next day as the Sharks boarded the plane to New Zealand.

We were on such a high, because the win against the Reds was the most points the Sharks had ever scored in Australia. I came off the bench and we gave them a thrashing – to the extent that I still remember it as one of the best games I ever played in. The guys threw the ball around and we played proper Sharks rugby at its best. That night we celebrated and the next day, Sunday, we were still happy as we waited to board the flight to Auckland. But when everybody else's boarding passes arrived, mine wasn't among them, and as we were going through security control they pulled me out and said, 'Sir, you don't have a visa to get into New Zealand.'

Our team manager, Trevor Barnes, started to negotiate, explaining that I was part of the team. What was the problem? Well, of course, the problem was that I was travelling on a Zimbabwean passport, which the Sharks hadn't experienced in Super Rugby before. South Africans didn't need a visa to get into New Zealand, but Zimbabweans did. So the officials said to Mr Barnes, 'You have to leave now, so you have two choices: you can go to Sydney and apply for an emergency visa, or you can go back to South Africa.'

Well, Mr Barnes immediately got on the phone and roused a few people back home and eventually it was confirmed that the two of us would fly to Sydney on Monday to apply for an emergency visa. When we got to the New Zealand consulate in Sydney, they asked some weird questions – whether I was part of the guerrilla warfare, and all sorts of horrific questions.

I said, 'What is this? I've never been involved in the military. I was born after independence, so what are you talking about?' Actually I was quite offended, but I had to practise some restraint because I wanted that visa. In fact, it was more like an interrogation than an interview and they made it clear that I had to leave on the date stated on the visa. But in the end they issued the visa and, after two days in Sydney, we were able to join the rest of the team in Auckland.

It turned out to be an incredible week, because it was my first time in New Zealand and I had always wanted to go. People said it was the toughest place to play and that winning there was not easy. Well, despite the fact that I hadn't trained all week due to being tied up in red tape in Australia, Dick picked me on the bench against the Blues and, with everything that had happened, I felt I wanted to prove myself all over again. Match day was typical Auckland weather, cold and wet, and in the end the difference between the two sides was the kicking of Percy Montgomery and Frans Steyn. Both teams scored three tries, but Frans knocked over two drop goals and we won 32–25.

South African teams haven't had a great record in Super Rugby in New Zealand, but the Sharks have always relished the challenge. I was excited by the passion the people there have for the game. A few people stopped me in the street because they had heard of this fellow called the Beast and it seemed to me that all the different age groups had one thing in common: they were informed and up to date with the game.

For the next game we travelled down to Hamilton and although we lost 35–27 to the Chiefs, we earned a bonus point for scoring four tries. That meant we took 10 log points from a month on the road and, with two wins and two defeats, that added up to a pretty successful tour.

When the Sharks got back to South Africa they had two games left in order to try to clinch a home semi-final: the Lions at home and the Stormers in Cape Town. There was a quantum leap in quality and Dick Muir's men took a full house of 10 points from the two games, winning 33–3 against the Lions at Kings Park and 36–10 at Newlands. In particular, the skill of two young players stood out; JP Pietersen on the wing and Frans Steyn, who Muir picked at wing, flyhalf and fullback in the course of the 2007 campaign. Both would go on to be key members of the Springbok World Cup winning team later the same year.

The dazzling finish to the Super Rugby season saw the Sharks make more history by becoming the first South African team to finish at the top of the table after the conclusion of log play. They met the Blues in the semi-final and won more comfortably than the 34–18 scoreline might suggest. More history followed as the Sharks became the first South African team to host a final since the competition was expanded from 10 to 12 in 1996. Moreover, in an unprecedented occurrence, it would be an all-South African final, the Bulls having beaten the Crusaders 27–12 in the other semi-final at Loftus Versfeld.

In contrast to the Sharks, the Bulls had endured a patchy first half of the season, losing four of their first nine games. On returning from Australasia, however, Heyneke Meyer's men found their mojo in spectacular fashion, demolishing the Stormers, Lions and Blues in successive weekends. This late surge opened up the mathematical possibility of reaching the semi-finals, but they needed to beat the Reds at Loftus by 44 clear points. That would see them leapfrog the Blues into third place. Few gave them a chance and fewer still admitted the possibility that a win by 72 points or more would move them one place further up the log and ensure a home semi-final.

In the event, the Bulls scored 13 tries against the hapless Reds and the final score of 92–3 set all kinds of records that still stand. Instead of the Bulls travelling to Christchurch to play the Crusaders, the defending champions had to go to Pretoria. Home advantage and the momentum created by a month of winning ensured a positive result and the Crusaders were downed 27–12, with all the Bulls' points coming from the boot of Derick Hougaard. The Sharks would host the Bulls in the grand final at Kings Park on Saturday, May 19th.

My phone started to ring on Saturday night, which is something I've got used to over the years. It's always people you don't talk to that much, a far-distant cousin who needs tickets all of a sudden, that kind of thing. But I also had to try to do the right thing for the friends I had made during my time in South Africa. The excitement around Durban was crazy; everywhere you went you saw Sharks posters. People came out in full force and the city became really busy. I was being stopped in the street and I guess it didn't help that I was now driving a big Nissan Navara with my name plastered all over it.

Dick wanted to do something a little different in the build-up to the game, so he got Henning Gerricke, a psychologist, to come and talk to us. It was a chance for the guys to open up and be honest, to voice how they were feeling and what they wanted to achieve. Henning wanted to make sure we weren't overwhelmed by the moment and Dick wanted us to all be in synch. And in the event, everything went well and we were properly prepared by the time the game kicked off. I was on the bench, as I had been for most of the season, and itching to get on.

Referee Steve Walsh missed a couple of vital things in the game. Bryan Habana tackled Percy Montgomery in the air and it should at the very least have been a yellow card, but the ref said play on and Percy was shaken up for the rest of the game. Then, immediately before Bryan scored the winning try, there was a ruck just outside our 22. I was right there and I saw the ball spill out towards our line, but Danie Rossouw picked up the ball (illegally) while he was lying on the ground and put it back in the ruck. So we're screaming, 'Knock-on!' but the ref and his assistants missed the knock-on and the penalty and this was all after the hooter had gone.

The crowd in the grandstand saw it and they were screaming so loud you couldn't hear yourself think, and I was wondering what was going on. But, anyway, the ball came back my way and I was in the defensive line about 10 metres from the try line as Habana came infield from the touchline. He straightened and there was about a 10-metre gap that had opened up between AJ Venter and me. We were all knackered – there was just nothing left to give. It was one of those moments when you feel like you're watching a movie and there's nothing you can do.

My abiding memory is of watching grown men cry. Bobby Skinstad, AJ Venter, Johann Muller and a few others; they were all crying. From my perspective, I wasn't that broken because I was a young man and I was thinking, 'I'm going to get another shot at this,' but here I am coming to the end of my career and it hasn't happened. At the time, though, I was going around the field trying to deal out some positive energy. I tapped JP Pietersen on the shoulder and gave Percy a hug, but one thing that didn't go down well was Jaco van der Westhuyzen celebrating by dangling from the crossbar and screaming at the top of his voice. By contrast, Bryan was very gracious; he came and shook everyone's hand.

Beast remembers the match being clearly in favour of the Sharks, but there were never more than four points dividing the sides until Albert van den Berg got over for the home team's second try in the 78th minute. Beast is correct about Habana's tackle on Percy Montgomery, however. The Springbok fullback took the hit in the second minute of the game and a yellow card seemed the obvious sanction. Perhaps because it was so early in the final, however, Steve Walsh opted for just a penalty.

Monty recovered to open the scoring with his first penalty of three on the day, but the Bulls grabbed the lead in the thirteenth minute with a try from Springbok eighth-man, Pierre Spies. The Bulls won a lineout in the Sharks' 22 and two rucks pulled in the Sharks defenders, allowing Victor Matfield to release Spies on a straight line to the score with a perfectly timed short pass.

Spies went from hero to zero five minutes later, when he over-elaborated at the back of a scrum on halfway and gifted possession to JP Pietersen. The left wing stretched away to score his twelfth try of the Super Rugby season and give the Sharks an 8–7 lead. Monty missed the conversion, but was successful with two more penalties, either side of one from Bulls flyhalf Derick Hougaard. It was 14–10 to the Sharks at the break and the general opinion was that they had not got full value on the scoreboard for the quality of their play.

The nerves endemic to finals rugby became apparent in the second half. There was no further scoring until Hougaard's 59th-minute penalty brought the Bulls within a point at 14–13. A full house of 54 000 at Kings Park was witnessing the closest final in the history of Super Rugby. The defining moment appeared to have arrived when Sharks lock Johann Muller soared high to win a lineout on the Bulls' 22. The resultant drive took play within five metres of the line. Beast was held up from the next drive, but replacement lock Albert van den Berg spotted daylight around the edge of the next ruck and dotted down 15 metres in from touch on the right-hand side.

In point of fact, however, the next action was the key to the last few frantic minutes. Frans Steyn took over kicking duties from Monty and, from a position he would expect to convert nine times out of ten, the precocious youngster pulled the ball wide of the left-hand upright. So instead of needing to score twice the Bulls, trailing 19–13, could win with a converted try.

In the last minute of regular time the Sharks made two crucial errors. First, flyhalf Butch James opted to launch an up-and-under from his own 10-metre line, gifting possession to the Bulls. That resulted in a run from right wing Akona Ndungane that was stopped in no-nonsense fashion on the halfway line. The tackler received the loudest shout of 'Beeaassttt!!' of the whole game.

The Bulls recycled the ball from the breakdown and then seemed to have ended their chances when hooker Gary Botha kicked the ball instead of passing. It was collected in the Sharks' 22 by Steyn, but instead of kicking it into the crowd, he sent it straight back whence it had come. It was that single moment that allowed the Bulls to build the winning platform. Matfield collected the ball and trotted up to halfway and the Bulls then moved from left to right across the half-way line, before releasing Habana down the right. He was tackled by Pietersen and, from the breakdown, Hougaard ran infield and fed replacement prop Danie Thiart.

This is where the game should have ended. Thiart was hammered in a double tackle and lost the ball towards the Sharks' line. Simultaneously, on the side of the ruck, Danie Rossouw fell with his back to the try line and, when he landed, scooped the ball back towards the arriving Bulls players who fell in a heap over it. YouTube footage clearly shows New Zealand referee Steve Walsh on one side of the ruck and his assistant Lyndon Bray on the other. Despite clear lines of sight, both missed the knock-on and the player on the ground playing the ball with his hands. To compound the error, Walsh allowed an unusually long time for the Bulls to make the ball playable again; many officials would have run out of patience and blown the full-time whistle long before Walsh said, 'There it is, half-back get it out.'

Instead the ball was carried one last time by the Bulls, first to the left, where Ndungane was stopped 10 metres short, and then to the right, where Habana received it a couple of metres in from touch and just inside the Sharks' 22. At this point we should acknowledge the genius of Bryan Habana. A few months later he would be awarded Player of the Tournament as the Springboks clinched their second World Cup and, at the moment of the 2007 Super Rugby final, he was at the absolute peak of his record-breaking career.

What separates the great from the good is the ability to seize the moment and, reviewing the footage from this distance, it is astonishing what Habana made from so little. When he received the ball on the end of a looped pass from scrumhalf Heinie Adams, there were 10 Sharks defenders clustered between him and the try line. He came infield apparently looking for support, and the majority of the defenders either held their position or crabbed towards the touchline, expecting play to come back their way. But as Habana sprinted alongside Beast, he suddenly pushed off his left foot and scythed through the gap between the prop and AJ Venter to the line. The clock read 81 minutes and 36 seconds. Amid the pandemonium, it took a further 90 seconds for Hougaard to slot the conversion that put the final score at 20–19 to the Bulls.

Sharks supporters have the moment etched forever on their souls. One of them, Durban-born Ted Docherty, had flown in from England just for the match and sent out a text saying, 'Does anyone know how to get the cork back into a champagne bottle?'

When we got back to the changing room John Plumtree and Dick were sitting there just staring into the distance. Nobody said anything at all for at least 15 minutes and I just sat there thinking,

'This could have been the greatest season of my life.'

Muir remembers the moment: 'The 2007 Super Rugby final still hurts me every time I see those Blue Bulls. That Sharks team was destined to go on and win that competition for a few years and what happened that day was devastating. Beast's contribution in the final was huge. We had to put it in perspective, but we lost the game and we should have gone on and been a dominant force in South Africa and Super Rugby for the next 10 years. But politics got in the way and instead of everybody being on the same page, we were pulling in different directions.'

Muir speaks with the benefit of hindsight, but for a young prop forward one door closing meant another opened.

Life goes on and the Currie Cup took over from Super Rugby. Most importantly for me, Deon Carstens was picked for the Boks to play two Tests against England and one against Samoa, so I was now the senior man at loosehead. I had really matured during Super Rugby and I now believed that the decision to move from the back row to the front was inspired. Of course, it helped that Dick reminded me about it every second day!

I had an outstanding Currie Cup in 2007, the cherry on top being when my parents came to watch me for the first time. They hadn't been able to get away for the Super Rugby final, but they had DStv and were able to watch me all through the season. My mum never doubted me, but my dad had only known academia as the way forward. He wanted the best for me, but I think it wasn't until he saw me on television that he realised he had been wrong and that I was a bit better as a sportsman than he had thought I was.

Chapter 6

FROM A SHARK TO A BOK

The only thing on my mind at the start of the 2008 season was establishing myself in the Sharks setup, but there was a new vibe at training because so many of my teammates had been part of the World Cup-winning Springbok team at the end of the 2007 season. To see those guys elevate their games to the next level and achieve greatness as a result was truly inspirational.

By the time I stepped up ahead of my second season in the Sharks setup I was energised. Reaching the final in 2007 had given me far more experience than I could have expected. My mission now was to become first choice, because I was playing behind Deon Carstens. As it turned out, though, Deon was injured during pre-season training and I simply stepped into his shoes. I played all the games and started in all but two. I ended up having one of my best seasons ever and I was among the nominees for SA Rugby Player of the Year.

At the beginning of May we needed bonus point wins in our last two home matches to reach the semi-finals and we did it in style, beating the Cheetahs 33–14 and the Chiefs 47–25. We scored seven tries against the Chiefs and after the game Peter de Villiers, the Springbok coach, came to see me. He asked whether my papers were in order and I said yes, that I qualified under the International Rugby Board (IRB) rule of having been in the country for three years. So he said, 'Well, get ready, because I want to use you in the June Test series.'

I was in shock! I was 22 and the only thing I was thinking about was playing as many games for the Sharks as possible and solidifying my position there. So I spoke to my mum and dad – I just couldn't wait to be a Springbok, but first the Sharks had to fly to Sydney to play the Waratahs in the semi-final. Actually, we came within one log point of having a home semi, but we failed to score enough tries during the season. We scored 32 in 13 games and 12 of those were in the last two. At the end of the season, Dick said, 'I was too conservative early on,' but it wasn't his fault.

In the end, we lost to the Waratahs and they went on to lose the final to the Crusaders. Shortly after flying back to South Africa, the Springbok squad was announced – and my name was in it! I was really excited and I couldn't wait for the first training session so that I could mix and mingle with the likes of Bakkies Botha and Victor Matfield. They had just come off winning a World Cup and those guys, together with the likes of Fourie du Preez, Schalk Burger, Bryan Habana and John Smit, were now legends of the game.

It helped that Beast played alongside Smit at the Sharks because the Bok captain recalls noticing him on an away trip the previous year. He says, 'I remember the first tour he came on with the Sharks to Australia. He was in transition from back row to prop and he was still trying to bulk up and I have never seen a guy eat the way he did. He would finish his own plate of ribs and then finish everything else that was left on everyone else's plate. He was on a mission; he knew what he had to do and he did it. It was the same with every aspect of his game; everything he was asked to do he did it plus more.'

I remember arriving for the first practice session and being so in awe of the legends that I was overwhelmed just to be in their presence. I looked around and saw guys laughing, but seeing Bizzy among them gave me confidence. We had played together so often that we were like brothers. My mission was to show Peter de Villiers that I could add value; I wanted to start a Test and define my position in the team.

At that first session Peter spoke to us about the plan for the two Tests against Wales and explained that he was going to name two different sides. In the first Test in Bloemfontein, Gurthrö Steenkamp and Brian Mujati were the two starting props, but in the second Test in Pretoria I got my chance in a front row made up entirely of the Sharks: BJ Botha, John Smit and Tendai Mtawarira.

In the week building up to the Loftus game, BJ took me under his wing and showed me the way. He guided me through what the Bok setup is all about and settled my nerves because I was constantly panicking, wondering whether there was a meeting I was missing, whether I was wearing the right kit, just reacting the way any eager young man would in a new environment. So it was pretty surreal, but I stuck with Bizzy as much as I could.

There was a lot of media attention around the fact that there were now two Zimbabwean props in the Springbok setup, Brian Mujati and me. Brian had been a year my senior at Peterhouse and made his debut a week before I did in the first Test against Wales. We had played Craven Week together in Pietermaritzburg in 2002, when I was still at Churchill. Brian was very talented, a real physical specimen with lots of potential.

In fact, there were three Zimbos in the squad, Tonderai Chavhanga being the third. He was two years older than me and when I was at Peterhouse he was one of the biggest stars to have come out of Zimbabwe. He played for the Stormers in 2004 and when the Super Rugby season was over he came back to Zimbabwe to share his experiences with a few of the schools. I remember leaning on him for advice at the Bok training camp because he had made his Test debut back in 2005 and set a record that has never been broken, scoring six tries on debut against Uruguay. All three of us qualified to play for South Africa through the IRB's three-year residency rule and at that stage there was no reason to suspect that trouble was coming.

There was no resentment from anyone about the three Zim guys because, I think, we all spoke one language: rugby. There were things going on in the wider world of South Africa, though, that certainly affected our psyche, specifically the xenophobic attacks in the townships. Tonderai was the first to speak out against it and he went to the media and we all spoke to Peter de Villiers, asking if there was something we could do. Peter felt it would be too much of a distraction from rugby so we were asked not to make a big thing about it.

One thing that people assumed was that Brian Mujati and I

were good mates simply because we went to the same school, but that wasn't the case.

I was kind of surprised at Brian's attitude and approach, because I believe he's one of the most talented individuals to have ever played in that position – tighthead. His physique was extraordinary and the jaws of guys like John Smit and Victor Matfield would drop when he took off his jersey, because he was built like a tank. He was so strong, very mobile, but just didn't have the right mindset.

Over the years, I've seen plenty of people who have had to learn the hard way that talent only takes you so far. So Brian's first year with the Boks was based purely on raw talent, but to stay up there for a long time takes a lot more than that. Ultimately, he gave up playing for the Boks, probably because he didn't want it enough. In that respect, we were not alike.

The day I made my debut I remember running out onto the field at Loftus, and linking arms with so many legends to sing the national anthem. Because they had won the World Cup, ours was a really settled team and I felt very fortunate to be one of the few new faces. Os du Randt retired after the World Cup final and that's what opened up a space for me in the squad.

We had beaten Wales 43–17 in Bloemfontein, but they made a few changes for the Pretoria Test and it was a much closer affair. In fact, their Lions winger Shane Williams scored a great long-range try after half an hour to give Wales the lead and it was 23–21 to the Boks with just over an hour of the game played. But then Jean de Villiers scored a try and Bizzy got one in the last minute and we finally won 37–21.

The next week we played Italy in Cape Town and it was in that game that I scored my first international try. It was a rainy day at Newlands and in the 55th minute Ricky Januarie put Bryan Habana into space; I managed to keep up with him as he drew the last defender and gave me the pass and I was able to score in the right-hand corner. It was a really special moment that capped an amazing start to my international career. Everything happened so quickly and all the while I was rubbing shoulders with the who's-who of the game.

Ahead of the Tri Nations, Peter said to me, 'You're going to get your chance, but now you have to show me that you want to start.' But then we went off to New Zealand and I wasn't even in the team. Gurthrö Steenkamp was the loosehead in Wellington and Dunedin, with me a non-playing reserve in the stands for both games. I went to Peter's hotel room in Wellington and said, 'Coach, I want to play,' and he said, 'Your turn is coming, just keep working hard.'

I was frustrated – I wanted to play.

As it turned out, we beat the All Blacks in Dunedin and then went to play the Aussies in Perth and Peter put me on the bench. He said, 'I'm going to give you your chance, but you must show me that you want to play.' The game was really tight and he put me on in the 53rd minute to replace Gurthrö; at that stage we were down 13–3 and I played my socks off. We were defending hard and I got a turnover, the ball moved from side to side and Jean de Villiers passed to me on the right wing, five metres from our try line. I ran around their hooker, Stephen Moore, and put in a 30-metre dash to the halfway line, then I passed to CJ van der Linde and we should have scored, but didn't. I had a few other good runs in the game; the team started playing better and I was really enjoying it. Peter said afterwards, 'I'm going to start you when we get back home.'

Finally, I got my chance in a friendly against Argentina at Ellis Park and we hammered them 63–9. The following week I started at Newlands against the All Blacks for the first time in my career, but we lost 19–0. The score didn't really reflect the game, because we scrummed them off the park, but we just couldn't score. In the dressing room after the game John Smit was furious, not because we'd lost, but because of the amount of support the All Blacks had from the home fans, the guys the media call the Cape Crusaders. They were going nuts for the All Blacks and John said that would be the last time we played at Newlands and that he would speak to Jurie Roux about it, that it was just unacceptable that this was happening in our own backyard.

The last two games of the Tri Nations were against Australia. They went on to beat us 27–15 in Durban, but we hammered them 53–8 in Johannesburg. It wasn't that we played badly in Durban, but in Joburg we just clicked – everything went our way; guys were finding each other and the centre pairing of Jean de Villiers and Adi Jacobs in particular was fantastic. At inside centre the Wallabies had Timana Tahu, who was a new superstar recruit from rugby league. There was so much talk about him before the match – that he was outstanding, a big hitter – but we just took him out of the game. His international union career was really over before it started and he ended up going back to league with his tail between his legs. I had a good game, some good runs and tackles, and we scrummed really well.

SA Rugby Annual *reported that 'a powerful Springbok scrum, led by loosehead Tendai "Beast" Mtawarira, buckled Australia's front row,' but the star of the game was left wing, Jongi Nokwe, who scored four of the eight Springbok tries. Some have compared the effect of this team performance to one played 11 years earlier at Loftus Versfeld. Again the opponent was Australia and this time the score was 61–22 to the Boks. It was Carel du Plessis's final game as Bok coach and his successor, Nick Mallett, inherited a team that had found its mojo. The Pretoria win was the first of a record-equalling 17 in a row. The 2008/9 team wasn't quite as dominant, but it won 10 of 11 Tests starting with the defeat of the Wallabies, and Beast now found himself an integral part of a team that had cause to fear no one in world rugby.*

After the Tri Nations, the Springbok players rejoined their unions for the closing stages of the 2008 Currie Cup. Without the likes of Beast, Bismarck and Jannie du Plessis, Ruan Pienaar, Butch James, JP Pietersen, Adi Jacobs and Odwa Ndungane, and with a string of injuries, the Sharks had to draw deep into their back-up squad at the beginning of the campaign. At one stage, coach John Plumtree said it was like going back to the days when rugby teams were selected 'by phoning the pub'. But they had an ace up their sleeve in French scrumhalf and flyhalf Freddie Michalak, who had been overlooked by his national selectors and played a full season of Super Rugby and Currie Cup for the Sharks.

What a man Freddie was. He was one of the most special

characters we've ever had in the Sharks setup. When he arrived he couldn't speak much English, but he said he had come to give himself to the team. I enjoyed Freddie for the kind of person he was on and off the field. On it he was tough as nails and would always give 110%; off it he would always make sure he spent time with the boys. Being an outsider, he made sure that he got to know everyone and he and I eventually became roommates, so we spent a lot of time together. His English got better and he was just a great human being.

The Sharks recovered from losing two of their first five games in the Currie Cup, and went on an 11-match unbeaten run, all the way to the final. The Blue Bulls were the opponents and, with Springboks aplenty on both sides, it was easy to think that this would be a re-run of the 2007 Super Rugby final. But this time there was no Habana-inspired great escape, and the Sharks hung on to win 14–9. It was their first Currie Cup title in 12 years, the last win having brought to an end a great era for the Sharks, who won four titles in seven seasons between 1990 and 1996. The team's achievements in 2007 and 2008 hinted that another great era might be underway. But there was no rest for Beast and the other Sharks Springboks, who gathered to fly to Britain for a three-Test tour. The first match against Wales was just a fortnight after the Currie Cup final.

We beat Wales 20–15 in Cardiff, then had a real scrap against Scotland in the wet at Murrayfield, winning 14–10 after being 10–0 down at half-time. But we finished the tour against England at Twickenham and that game was one where it all clicked. We won 42–6, at the time the worst defeat England had ever suffered against any opponent at Twickenham as well as the most points anyone had ever scored against them there. Nigel Owens was the referee and he gave me a yellow card that was really unfair. There was a ruck and someone was holding the ball in and not letting it out, but it wasn't me! So there I was in the sin-bin, stressing that Peter de Villiers wouldn't let me back on, but he had to, I was playing really well. I remember that we smashed England in the scrums and one of the casualties of the result was Danny Cipriani, who was dropped for the next game and didn't get back into the side for a decade.

Chapter 7

THE CREST OF A WAVE

At the end of the Sharks' 2008 Super Rugby campaign, Dick Muir joined the Springboks as assistant to coach Peter de Villiers. John Plumtree took over the coaching of the Currie Cup side and in 2009 he followed Muir into the coaching seat for Super Rugby. Plumtree, a New Zealander by birth, was a back-row forward for the Sharks in the early 1990s and had been part of the coaching setup for several years before taking over from Muir. For most of the players, Beast included, it was pretty much business as usual.

The 2009 season was the first with John Plumtree as head coach. Plum was a great coach in his own right and he fed off the environment that Dick had already put in place, so in many ways things just carried on the way they had been at the Sharks. Plum, though, was a lot stricter than Dick – it's fair to say everything was a little more relaxed with Dick around – but he proved to be more like a father figure to me and indeed to most of the young guys. Players such as JP Pietersen, Waylon Murray and Bismarck du Plessis all came through under Plum. We knew that if we were naughty, we would get a slap across the back of the hand to put us back in line, but we also knew that if you did well you'd be rewarded.

That's the way Plum worked and we respected him for it and made sure we did our jobs. If there was one thing he brought to the mix it was a little more physicality; he believed that that was very important and our forwards grew as a result, particularly us youngsters. During 2009 the Sharks became quite the feared pack in Super Rugby. I was 23 now and after my first season in the Springboks I found that opposition teams began to target me. Especially at scrum time, they would come up with tricks. The Aussie and Kiwi teams would make a point of telling the press in the week ahead of their Sharks game that they had plans in place to nullify me.

Ultimately, it made me work harder and it helped having a guy like Bizzy next to me, because he pushed me a lot. He never allowed me to rest on my laurels and that was important, because when you make it as a Springbok that can sometimes be easy and Bismarck never let that happen to me. He was always on my case, making sure he brought out the best in the Beast. And when his older brother, Jannie du Plessis, joined the Sharks in 2009, Jannie also became a mentor; we used to call him the 'scrum guru', because he always seemed to know everything happening up front and his knowledge was valid.

A number of other players who had helped me in the transition from back row to front row were also still around, so there was a lot of correction from week to week. Because fatigue sets in, sometimes it's easy to forget the basics and you stop paying attention to them. Balie always made me watch my game afterwards and he would point out where my back was not straight enough, my feet were too far back, my bind was not strong enough, my hips were out; stuff like that. All these guys made me work harder.

Bizzy was like a brother to me. He was already at the Sharks when I was still coming through at the Academy and we played a lot of rugby together for the Under-21s. He was a tough guy, a real hard nut, who was hungry and wanted things his way. He set the bar high and always strived to be the best, so when he first moved to the Sharks he must have struggled to relate. He had a strong personality and a no-nonsense approach, but sometimes in a rugby setup you need to know how to relax and I think Bizzy struggled with that. Because he was so driven, he battled to put a smile on his face.

Perhaps it was because we had played so much junior rugby together, but I felt I was the one guy who understood Bismarck. When Jannie arrived, he slotted in at tighthead and we became a brotherhood. As a front row, we ended up playing over 50 Tests together and more than 80 Super Rugby games, and obviously got to know each other's games really well. But from day one we got into the habit of giving each other positive criticism; Jannie would point things out to me, I would do the same for him, and Bizzy would tell us both where we were going wrong!

All of this became second nature to us because we played together so often and I was perhaps the one person in the Sharks setup who truly understood them. Both Bizzy and Jannie were big personalities and controlled a lot of what happened at the

Sharks. They would always speak out if they felt strongly about something.

The 2009 campaign was a case of so near and yet so far. After eight rounds, the Sharks led the overall log, with seven wins to their name, including three on the road in Australasia. They then lost four of their last five games to finish sixth. The final game against the Bulls at Kings Park offered a last chance to make the playoffs, but the Sharks needed to win with a four-try bonus point to progress. They got the four tries, but lost the match by the slenderest of margins, 27–26.

So, despite a great start, the Sharks didn't make the playoffs in Super Rugby, but personally I had a really good tournament. Throughout my career I have never really thought much about the Springboks at the beginning of the year, because I know that I have to give all my attention to the Sharks. I believe that in order to play for the Springboks I have to play well for the Sharks and, in that way, I try to keep at bay any thoughts of entitlement. If I play well, week in and week out, then eventually the Bok coach – whoever he may be – has to look at me. But 2009 was a little different, because it was a British and Irish Lions year.

For me, playing against the British and Irish Lions is the next best thing to a World Cup. I would say that South Africans relish it more than they do playing against individual countries. Spectators from overseas come out in numbers to support the Lions and the hype was already there in Super Rugby 2009; the Lions tour was that important. It was all over the media and we were told that this Lions team was the best since the one that had beaten us here in 1997. They had big stars, guys such as Brian O'Driscoll and Paul O'Connell, and I had to pinch myself to think I was going to be part of that series.

The week before the first Test, in Durban, the Springboks sat down and watched a video of what the Lions players had been saying about our forwards. They basically said we weren't good enough as a pack to go up against the Lions pack. They put up stats about Phil Vickery and Andrew Sheridan – how they bench pressed ridiculous weights – and then they started badmouthing players in our team and, in particular, me. I was too inexperienced, they said, and they also had a go at John Smit for the same reason, because he had moved from hooker to tighthead for the series. The reason was that Bizzy was playing so well at hooker that he had to play, but they also couldn't drop John because he was captain, so they moved John to tighthead.

John Smit remembers the same video. 'All three of us – Beast, Bizzy and myself – were being talked down quite hard by the Lions players and management and they were expecting to obliterate us. So we got ourselves more and more worked up ahead of the game with every negative article or comment. It's the most worked up the three of us have ever been and on the day, of course, Beast almost single-handedly ended Phil Vickery's international career.'

After we had watched the video, Victor Matfield came to me and said, 'Don't even worry what they're saying in the media. Just know that we got you. Do your job and we'll push behind you.'

Those words really calmed me down, because I won't lie, I was nervous. During the week the hype became extraordinary and there were red jerseys everywhere you went in Durban. But, with the help of Victor and others, I was able to put aside the noise and get down to training really hard.

On Tuesday we had a full-on training session in the forwards and scrummed against the guys on the bench. It was really intense and replicated the match situation perfectly. The funny thing was that John hadn't played prop since he was an Under-21, but he adapted to tighthead really well, with a lot of advice from Bismarck. That session really set us up and from then on it was pretty much muscle memory. I don't believe the Lions trained as hard as we did and they were complacent. They believed the hype that they were better than us.

When match day came we were ready and all the emotions we had been feeling through the week came to the surface at the first scrum. It was on the right-hand touchline and the Lions didn't know what hit them. The ball came in and I went berserk. The push really came through from behind and I remember the energy I felt. Bizzy did his job really well and didn't allow Vickery to come into my space. I went up and saw Phil's legs go up in the air and I remember the emotion I felt after the scrum. I was pumped up and just went nuts; I had fire in my eyes and was ready to kill him. The crowd went wild; Vickery didn't know what had hit him and his eyes were the size of dinner plates.

From then on it just got worse at every successive scrum. I could see he was hurting and that wasn't surprising because we were getting stuck into him properly. It's tough because as a player you never set out to break someone's spirit, but inevitably you do. From my perspective, I just wanted to show who I was. I was saying, this is me and you didn't respect me before, but you're going to respect me now. He lasted until half-time and was then pulled off five minutes into the second half and we could see that he was crying. He was broken; I doubt whether he had experienced anything like that in his whole career.

We were so prepared for him; it wasn't just me acting on my own – the whole tight five must take credit and the back-row boys played their part too. It was a great day at the office and after the game it seemed like the whole of the British media contingent wanted to speak to me. They wanted to know how this youngster got to ruin the career of a legend and, to tell the truth, it went to my head. I got complacent, feeling like I'd done enough.

The second Test was the following week in Pretoria and the Lions started Welshman Adam Jones at tighthead. He was a good scrummager and I went in with the wrong attitude. I kind of took my foot off the pedal. I did okay, but not great – definitely not as good as the first Test. The Lions wanted that game so badly, so they came out aggressively and hit us hard in the contact, pushing them 19–8 ahead after an hour. There was a moment just after half-time where we started to believe in ourselves again, though. Bakkies cleaned out Adam Jones at a ruck and he couldn't carry on. He was replaced and we rallied around Bakkies, who got a two-week ban for his pains. Remember that most of our team were World Cup winners and in tough times we always had that belief to fall back on. There was so much experience there and such strong leadership, and of course the first Test result was key. The fight-back came when Bryan Habana scored and we moved ahead for the first time when Jaque Fourie ran over Ronan O'Gara to score in the corner.

The match – and series – was won in injury time when Morné Steyn kicked a penalty from our own half and we knew right away that we had achieved something massive. In the final Test the Lions beat us comfortably 28–9, but no one remembers that; they just remember the two we won. Phil Vickery returned as the starting tighthead and he actually got the better of me in that game. I think there was a touch of complacency on my part, thinking that I had already done the job, and I was also a little tired. I hadn't expected the coach to start me in all three Tests, but he did and Gurthrö Steenkamp only saw a total of 25 minutes off the bench in the series.

Victory in the Lions series was the harbinger for more silverware in the Tri Nations. Since the inception of the Tri Nations in 1996, the Boks had only won it twice; once in 1998 under the coaching of Nick Mallett and again in 2004, Jake White's first season as Springbok coach. The tournament had been dominated by New Zealand and they were regarded as favourites, having produced three of the semi-finalists in Super Rugby. Significantly, however, the one non-Kiwi team in the last four became the 2009 champions, the Bulls winning their second title after breaking Sharks supporters' hearts in 2007.

The 2009 Springbok Tri Nations squad featured 28 players, 10 of them Bulls, 11 of them Sharks, with the bulk of the first-choice 15 being World Cup winners from 2007. There were still critics who would claim that the Boks were lucky at that World Cup, that they had managed to avoid New Zealand and Australia, and that they were short of real quality. Any doubt about that quality was dispelled in seven glorious weeks, however, as the Boks marched to their third title. Along the way, they beat New Zealand three times in a row, a feat that they had last achieved in 1949 and have not come close to replicating since.

After the Lions series we, as a squad, were on a high and when the Tri Nations series came around it was like living a dream. We had such a good team that I was able to enjoy the ride and the three wins in that series against the All Blacks are right up there with my greatest achievements. We started off against New Zealand in Bloemfontein and an awesome try from Ruan Pienaar got us going. We imposed ourselves physically and hurt the All Blacks in the contact. The scrums were really good, but what gave us the edge was our driving maul. Around that time Victor Matfield was one of the best rugby players in the world and he was the mastermind at lineout time.

Having won in Bloemfontein, we knew we had the All Blacks' number. You could feel it in the camp and the way we trained and interacted. We knew we were a formidable team, but we never let it get to our heads. We made sure we stayed humble – one thing with John as captain was the calming effect and leadership that he brought. He knew how to say the right things at the right time.

When we went to Durban for the second Tri Nations Test we knew we had the All Blacks rattled and we fed off that and punished them again. Morné Steyn scored all 31 of our points and we defended like Trojans. I remember getting my hands on the ball from a kick-off and making a nice break. I moved round their winger, Sitiveni Sivivatu, and he couldn't catch me. Piri Weepu had to come across to tackle me, otherwise I would have been clean through. I was having lots of fun, enjoying the fact that we were playing great rugby.

At Newlands we beat Australia 29–17, with Victor scoring a great try. John Smit was carrying the ball near halfway and there was no one close enough to support him, so he dummied a long pass to the wing and then dropped the ball on his foot and put through the most perfect grubber. The Wallabies were so shocked that they didn't know what to do and Victor trotted through, grabbed the ball and scored.

We had two weeks off after the Newlands game before we travelled to Perth to play the Wallabies again. We won that game 32–25, scoring four tries, but then lost 21–6 in Brisbane a week later. We had an off day, but there was a Zimbabwean on both sides, with David Pocock having a great game for Australia in his debut season in the Tri Nations. He had a huge effect on the game and was one of the key reasons for our defeat.

Even though we had already beaten them twice, no one expected us to win against the All Blacks in New Zealand, and we travelled to Hamilton needing to win to make us Tri Nations champions for only the third time. The whole week there was a buzz in the team because we knew the significance of the occasion. There were just a few guys who had won it under Jake White in 2004, but for most of us this was to be a new experience.

The game was played at a high intensity, with us defending most of the time as they shifted us left and right, which is something that most New Zealand teams try to do. There were a couple of moments that stood out, the first being when Frans Steyn kicked a penalty from our own 10-metre line. That's when the Kiwis got really scared: they knew that they couldn't even give away penalties in their own half because Frans was still going to kick it over. And he went on to get two more in the first 30 minutes, both from inside our own half. The moment that secured the game, I think, was when Jean de Villiers got an intercept try in the 51st minute. And when the final whistle blew and we had won 32–29, there was some relief mingled with the ecstasy.

Chapter 8

MAN OVERBOARD

The Sharks lost to the Cheetahs in the Currie Cup semi-final on October 17th, which gave Beast a couple of weeks off to recharge his batteries ahead of the Springboks' end-of-season tour to Europe. What he did not suspect was the extent of the problem brewing behind the scenes with members of South Africa's ruling party, the African National Congress (ANC). Beast was about to become a political football. He was duly selected for the tour, but the same week, Oregan Hoskins, the president of the South African Rugby Union (Saru) received a fateful call.

Hoskins, officially known as Oregan, but more familiarly as Regan, was president of Saru for 10 years. He had previously served as the president of the KwaZulu-Natal Rugby Union (KZNRU) and put his job with a legal practice in Durban on hold to serve Saru full time. He resigned in 2016 and now works as a magistrate in Pietermaritzburg.

He recalls the moment when his phone rang and the name that came up on the screen was that of the South African Deputy

Minister of Sport and Recreation, Gert Oosthuizen: 'Just before the end-of-year tour in 2009, I got a call at home on a Sunday afternoon.

'Gert said he wanted to talk to me about Beast. He said, "The Minister [Reverend Makhenkesi Stofile] has asked me to tell you that you will not pick Beast for the tour." I asked why, because by this point Tendai had already played 19 Tests for the Springboks over two seasons. I said, "Why are you making this an issue?" and he said, "Because he is not a South African citizen."

'I should just add at this point that Gert had been extremely helpful to me personally and to rugby in South Africa. I think being an Afrikaner and an ex-rugby player (as he claims to be) helped and the one time he let rugby down was on this issue. I got the firm impression that he was fully in support of his Minister regarding Beast.

'I said, "I understand the citizenship issue because I'm a lawyer, but I cannot accept this. How do I tell this young man that he cannot play for South Africa when you do not have a legal case, either as the Ministry of Sport or as government?" Gert claimed that the Sports Act states that you must be a citizen to represent South Africa and I said, "No, it doesn't. I know the Act back to front; I've read it and studied it and your regulations have not even been promulgated because they would be unconstitutional. That's why you as a government have never published them."

'We had a massive argument and he would not listen to reason. He insisted that between government, the Minister of Sport and himself, we would not play Beast. I told him, "I'm very angry because you are putting me and rugby in a predicament. I understand that, politically, rugby is still seen as a white sport and I represent that *sport, so the last thing I am going to do is cause problems with the ANC and government. Rugby is not in a position to stand its ground. If I were the president of the South African Football Association (SAFA), I would have done so. I would have told you to f*** off, but I know that as rugby I can't." So we had a full-on slanging match on the phone, but in the end I had to put the phone down to Gert and call Beast.*

'I had never phoned him before, but now I did and I said, "Tendai, you need to come and see me, it's very important." And he found my place, which is not easy; it's in a valley in Westville [near Durban]. So he sat in my house and I told him, "The Minister of Sport has just ordered me not to pick you." And he just burst out crying. It was really heart-wrenching, because I liked Tendai from day one, from the time when he moved down to Durban. I was president of KZNRU at the time and I saw this kid coming from Peterhouse, playing loose forward, being moved by Dicky to prop and making a success of it.

'The reason I valued him so highly was that he was a foreign kid who did not have the luxury of a rich father, like a Bryan Habana or a Schalk Burger, for instance, standing there at the side of the field literally easing the aches and pains they get from rugby. Tendai had nobody, literally nobody, and he had made a success of it. And here was this massive guy, sitting in my house, crying his heart out, and I thought that I was responsible.

'I tried my best to talk to him and assure him that I would do my best to get his citizenship, but he just couldn't understand why he couldn't go on tour. I said, "Do yourself a favour and don't make an issue of this; drop the tour and I'll help you with citizenship." I

didn't know how, but I thought I had the answers at that time. As a lawyer I thought I had a handle on it, but didn't realise how difficult citizenship was to get. It was one of the most unpleasant experiences I had in rugby.'

Perhaps backing Hoskins's legal opinion, effectively Saru now called government's bluff. Beast joined the Springbok squad in Fourways in Johannesburg and remained in full training while the politicians argued. On Saturday, November 7th, Saru released a statement saying that Beast had been cleared to tour with the Bok squad following 'productive discussions' with the Sports Ministry. Saru was alerted to clauses in the National Sport and Recreation Amendment Act, 2007, which needed to be completed before he could tour.

Hoskins stated in the release, 'We are delighted with the news after discovering this problem during the week. The government has been very helpful in expediting the completion of the necessary protocols and we're all relieved that Beast will be available for selection for the Springboks against France in Toulouse on Friday.'

The decision had been made for the Boks to remain in South Africa until the last possible moment, before flying to France for the first Test, which was – unusually, for an international match – played on a Friday night. The team left Johannesburg on Wednesday night, arriving in France on Thursday morning. On the same day, however, the Sports Minister made an about-turn. A press release (complete with some idiosyncratic emphases) by Sport and Recreation South Africa on November 12th stated:

The problems encountered by Mr Mtawarira with his

Zimbabwe passport have exposed a dangerous situation; a situation where sport administrators clearly do not know South African laws or simply do not respect our laws.

We must state up front our admiration for the gifted Zimbabwean prop forward. He is a live wire on the rugby field. But just like he must obey the rules of rugby on the field, he must comply with the laws of South Africa in life here on our land, like all of us.

According to the President, as well as the chief executive officer of the South African Rugby Union (SARU), The Beast IS NOT A CITIZEN of South Africa. He does not even have a permit for permanent residence in South Africa. The chief executive officer of The Sharks corroborates these facts and makes the interesting remarks: 'There has never been any issue about his nationality.'

The issue here is NOT nationality. It is his citizenship. He has never applied for a South African citizenship or passport. Of course he would not get a passport if he was not our citizen. This is the law that all citizens in all countries respect. What is wrong with some of our compatriots? No sport can be bigger than South Africa!

The officials of the SARU even inform us that Mr Mtawarira is currently on an exceptional-skills visa (work permit). If such a work permit was issued on the basis of his skills as a prop forward, the concept scarce skills was vulgarised. The Sharks or any provincial unit or professional club may motivate for the issuing of a work permit for a limited number of foreign players or administrators. Such

84

application must be accompanied by a COMPELLING motivation.

Most important still, sports leaders should be the first to understand why NATIONAL TEAMS cannot play foreigners, no matter how outstanding they may be. Morné Steyn cannot represent New Zealand, Dan Carter cannot represent Wales, and Wayne Rooney cannot play for Bafana Bafana. The list goes on.

Federations, provinces and clubs are more than welcome to approach us for advice on these issues. To simply rely on slipping through the legal framework (as the chief executive officer of The Sharks seems to be doing) is very dangerous and negligent. Let us take our country more seriously. Only citizens of a country may represent that country.

Saru's response was that they 'noted' the statement, but referred the press to their own of the previous Saturday. As far as they were concerned, there was no issue and Beast duly took his place in the match-day team in Toulouse. An element of farce was added to proceedings when the South African national anthem was sung. A reggae musician by the name of Ras Dumisani, born in Durban but resident in France since 1992, rendered a tone-deaf and incoherent version of 'Nkosi Sikelel' iAfrika' as the Boks lined up. Schalk Burger and Victor Matfield, in particular, were visibly angry at the cheapening of the anthem and on Sunday an official complaint was laid. There was a full inquest into how and why Dumisani was booked in the first place.

In many ways, this was the final straw in what had been a trying week for the squad and it was not entirely surprising to see them go down 20–13 to a ferocious French display. Hoskins missed the Test, but caught up with the team in Udine and it was in this ancient city, close to Italy's north-eastern border with Slovenia, that the Saru president and Gert Oosthuizen, Deputy Minister of Sport, met face to face.

Hoskins recalls: 'Gert pitched up at the team hotel and said he wanted to chat. I should reiterate that we had always had a good relationship. We spent a lot of time together at the 2007 World Cup, went to restaurants in Paris, drank wine, got on well. When he arrived at the hotel I was with Mark Alexander, my deputy president at Saru, and we were given a meeting room to chat.

'I went crazy and lost all respect. I accused him and the Minister of total bigotry. I used every bad word under the sun. I'm amazed he didn't react, because I felt like taking the table and throwing it at him; that's how angry I was. I pointed out to him that the Sports Act does not prescribe that the Minister has powers to tell a sports body who they may and may not pick. I reiterated the fact that nowhere within the Act was there any mention of the requirement for South African citizenship.

'I then went on to give him a list of Zimbabweans and Namibians who had played for South Africa, because I had done my homework. I showed him the list and then I said, "You know what the sad part is, Gert? They're all white players. Now for the first time we have a black Zimbabwean and you and your Minister are saying that we can't pick him. But the precedent has been set; the Beast has already played 20 Tests."

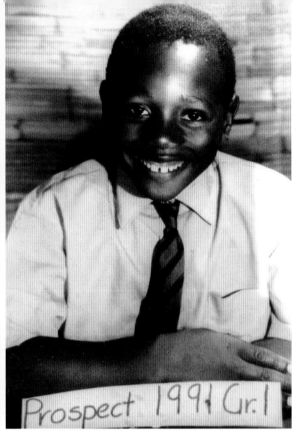

LEFT: My first year at Prospect Primary School.
(© Mtawarira family collection)

BELOW: The Peterhouse heads of houses in 2004 in their blue blazers. Back row (left to right): Bavin Parikh, Tinashe Nyambo. Front row (left to right): Nyasha Chimokoto, Pete de Klerk, Mr Madondo, Allan Mudawarira and Tendai Mtawarira (in a blazer two sizes too small!).
(© Mtawarira family collection)

ABOVE: Captain of the first team at Peterhouse in 2004. In the middle is coach Paul Davies.
(© Mtawarira family collection)

BELOW: Back row (left to right): my mum-in-law, Margaret, Mrs Munyenyiwa and my mum, Bertha. Bottom row (left to right): Mr Munyenyiwa, me and my dad, Felix.
(© Mtawarira family collection)

ABOVE LEFT: It's all his fault! Dick Muir, the man who persuaded me to become a prop. (© Steve Haag)

ABOVE RIGHT: Balie Swart, the man who made me a prop and, coincidentally, the Springbok tighthead when we won the World Cup in 1995. (© Steve Haag)

BELOW: Two of my mentors showing me the ropes as I transition from back row to front row, Kings Park, 2007. Deon Carstens on the left, John Smit in the middle. (© Steve Haag)

ABOVE: 'Now, Son, let me tell you a couple of things about scrumming.' One of my mentors, Sharks and Springbok tighthead, BJ Botha. (© Steve Haag)

BELOW: Celebrating my first Currie Cup final win. Sharks 14–9 Blue Bulls, Kings Park, 2008. (© Steve Haag)

ABOVE: My first Test, against Wales at Loftus Versfeld, June 2008. Ryan Kankowski is about to crush an unfortunate Welshman, watched by Juan Smith. (© Steve Haag)

BELOW: Things are about to get uncomfortable for Phil Vickery as the British and Irish Lions tighthead scrums down against me. (© Steve Haag)

ABOVE: Carrying the ball against the Lions, Kings Park, 2009. Lions scrumhalf Mike Phillips looks on. (© Steve Haag)

BELOW: Celebrating the series win against the Lions, 2009. (© Steve Haag)

Scrumming down with my brothers, Bismarck (middle) and Jannie du Plessis, against England at Twickenham, 2014. (© Steve Haag)

The Beast on Oxford Street. Outside the Asics Store in London. (© Steve Haag)

'I even went on to say about Corné Krige being born in Zambia, Gary Teichmann being from Zimbabwe, and both captained the Springboks during the last decade. He wouldn't budge. He said, "The Minister says he's a Zimbabwean. Government backs him and Beast's not going to play for South Africa." I said, "What about soccer? Every team in South Africa is full of foreigners and some have played for Bafana Bafana." I tried every argument, but I knew it was going to fall on deaf ears. I was shouting and screaming.'

Somehow, the 'gentlemen's agreement', as Hoskins calls it, held. Beast was allowed to stay on tour and was unaware of the political drama unfolding in the background; he played 20 minutes off the bench against Italy and started the final game against Ireland at Croke Park in Dublin. A subdued Bok performance saw them lose 15–10 in front of a massive crowd of 75 000. Beast was not to know it, but his 22nd Test for South Africa would be his last for almost a year.

Chapter 9

THE DARKEST HOUR

In January 2010, Butana Komphela, an ANC MP and chairman of government's Sports Committee, accused Saru of 'illegally' fielding Beast. 'The government is going to punish rugby,' said Komphela. 'We are going to charge SA Rugby for fielding a foreign national without proper requirements. The portfolio committee has inquired as to why Beast is still playing for South Africa if he is a foreign national. It is a contravention of the laws. The government will deport him to Zimbabwe. He is here on a work permit and he is flouting it. We have no problem with him playing for the Sharks, but this doesn't mean he has acquired citizenship.'

For the first and only time in the whole sorry business, Beast responded publicly. He said, 'I am a South African at heart. I love this country. It has become my home. It is everything to me. Wearing the green and gold of the Springboks is a huge honour for me. That jersey is part of me. The green and gold flows in my blood.'

Recalling the emergence of the ANC firebrand, Hoskins says, 'Butana Komphela's statements were utterly xenophobic. I spoke to him and to Gert, but for some reason I never got the chance to speak directly to Minister Stofile. He never once came to watch the Springboks play and I invited him every time. I had met him in the past and he had always been very amiable towards me, right up until March 2008 when his brother, Mike Stofile, stood against me for the presidency of Saru.'

Beast had been advised to keep his head down and to allow the politicians to sort it out, so he devoted his attention to the Sharks' Super Rugby campaign. But some time around the beginning of May 2010 he received a call from Hoskins.

Regan said that he didn't believe it was anything personal against me, but that the Minister was targeting rugby. He said the Minister was angry with Saru and trying to use whatever he could to punish the sport. So Regan was doing his job to make me aware of what was happening behind the scenes and I just carried on playing, believing all the time that they would resolve it and it would just go away.

Hoskins announced the Springbok squad for the June internationals on May 22nd. It was the day of the Super Rugby semi-finals, both being played in South Africa.

The Bulls hosted the Crusaders at Orlando Stadium in Soweto in the first game and the Stormers played the Waratahs at Newlands. The Sharks had lost their first five matches of the season and, although they then won seven of their last eight, it wasn't enough to reach the last four.

No one had contacted me since that call from Regan in May so I just kind of assumed that things had been resolved. I was in Margate, on the South Coast with my fiancée when the squad was announced and my name wasn't there. I remember literally breaking down and crying in front of my wife-to-be. I had just had the season of my career in 2009 and things were looking up, I was feeling great and I simply couldn't understand what had happened. The first thing I did was call Regan and he said, 'Beast, this is difficult for me to say, but you've been left out because the Minister of Sport is blocking you from playing for the Boks.'

My fiancée had to help me back to my feet and the first thing we did was pray for guidance and direction. I called my mum and dad. My dad was furious and my whole family was angry and upset about the way the situation was being handled. Finally, after a couple of days, it began to sink in that I was actually not part of the team. The Boks flew back from Wales and gathered in Cape Town ahead of the French Test and Peter de Villiers asked me to fly down and come and see him. So I did.

Peter said, 'We need to devise a plan. Obviously the situation right now is that I can't pick you. It makes me very upset because I want to use you, you're in my plans, but I can't. What we need to do is get you the best Home Affairs person possible to help us.'

At the time I was carrying a work visa valid for three years and was travelling on my Zim passport. There was a woman at the Home Affairs office in Morningside who had been helping me ever since I first came to South Africa. Her name was Michelle; I met her when I was a 19-year-old and to this day she does everything for my family. She was tasked with sorting out my South African passport, but she was just overwhelmed. She told me from the outset that it could take six years. She said that the situation at that time at Home Affairs was very difficult and that there was so much red tape; that there was no way to get around it and we would have to go through the process. In other words, we had to wait.

In my head I was thinking there was no way I was going to wait six years for a passport. I won't be in the form I am in now if I wait for that long to play for the Boks. I spoke to John Plumtree, who had taken over from Dick Muir as the Sharks coach, and he told me to go overseas. 'Stuff them for treating you like this.' And he wasn't alone. Many people, close friends and family included, told me to leave. 'You can't be treated like this after the way you've performed.' So I would be lying if I said it didn't cross my mind to leave and play overseas, but I never got to the stage of contacting clubs, because I knew deep down that my heart was here.

On June 5th, 2010, the Springboks played Wales in Cardiff, winning 34–31. On the same day, Saru issued a statement that read, 'The Springbok selectors have been instructed by the South African Rugby Union not to select Tendai "Beast" Mtawarira – or any other non-South African passport holder – for the national team, following communication from the Department of Sport and Recreation.

'Saru received a letter on Friday from Deputy Sports Minister, Mr Gert Oosthuizen, reaffirming the government's position that no foreign player can be selected to represent a national team.

'The Zimbabwean-born Mtawarira has played 22 Test matches for the Springboks since his debut in 2008. He is legally resident and employed in South Africa and was selected to play for the Springboks having fulfilled the eligibility criteria of the International Rugby Board.

*'"We have had extensive and robust conversations with govern-
ment on this issue," said Mr Oregan Hoskins, president of Saru.
"But we respect the authority of the Ministry and have instructed
our selectors in that regard."*

*'Mr Hoskins added that Mtawarira wished to become a South
African citizen as soon as possible and Saru had been assisting him
in fulfilling the necessary criteria.'*

With all this stuff being thrown at me, I needed to escape, so I
went and hid myself in a little box, away from everything. I spoke
to my fiancée and she asked me what I felt and where my heart
really was. My answer to that question was and has always been
the same till this very day – I told her, 'My heart is here and I want
to play for the Boks and the Sharks. I love this country and I want
to contribute so much more. This is just the beginning.'

So we prayed about it and made a decision that whatever
it took I would get that South African passport. We prayed for
opportunity and for the right people to come along. So, while the
June Tests were being played, I took the time to visit Regan at his
house in Durban. We spoke at length about how we could possibly
fix the situation. During the same time I was watching the Boks
play and I must say, they were playing some good rugby. Gurthrö
Steenkamp had taken over my position. He had an amazing performance in the Test against France and I was happy for him, but
inside it also hurt, because I wasn't there to defend my jersey.

*Hoskins finally took a decision to escalate matters, but he
didn't tell Beast. He says, 'I had met Minister Nkosazana Dlamini-
Zuma at the South African embassy in France during the World
Cup in 2007. [Dlamini-Zuma was then Minister of Foreign Affairs,*

but was shuffled to Home Affairs in May 2009.] At that point Mike Stofile was still deputy president of Saru and he came with me. Jesse Duarte was also there, but she couldn't care less. But Nkosazana was asking me a lot of questions and for some reason she gave me her phone number and now it came in handy.

'So when Beast was formally banned from playing for the Springboks, I messaged her and said, "Madam, I need to meet with you about Beast." She messaged me back and said to come and see her at her house. Her house was at the Zimbali Golf Estate in Ballito and when I arrived on the Sunday she was having afternoon tea with a lady who then excused herself. I said, "We are in a serious impasse here with Beast. We need him in the team because there's a World Cup coming up in 18 months' time. I've been told by the Minister of Sport not to pick him and the only solution is to sort out his citizenship."

'At that point I had done lots of background work. I had been several times to see Michelle, Beast's contact at Home Affairs, and she had told me it could take between six and ten years to process his application because of all the red tape. That was not good enough for me – we needed it and we needed it now! So I said to the Minister, "I've had a look at the Act and you are the only one who can fast track this process." She listened to me and said that government was concerned about South Africans not getting jobs and so on and so forth. But even so, she said she would consider it, and to her credit it wasn't long – maybe a week or two – before she phoned me and said, "I've considered it and I'm going to give him citizenship."'

While Hoskins was working on Beast's behalf, the man himself was starting to lose hope.

During those three weeks when the Boks were playing at home and I was shuttling between Regan and Michelle at Home Affairs, I started to think that this was probably not going to work out. But at the very moment when I was about to give up, I received a phone call that changed everything. I got a call from a friend saying, 'Hey, Beast, the Arch wants to speak to you. Make sure your phone is on.'

Later that afternoon my phone rang, I answered and a voice said, 'Is that Beast? It's the Arch here.' It was none other than Archbishop Desmond Tutu on the line. He said, 'I love what you do for South Africa. Every time you get the ball the crowd shouts, "Beeaaassst!" and I think it's fantastic. You're a great ambassador and a role model, you represent us and this whole thing that's happened to you is unfair and unjust.'

I was surprised that the Arch even knew about me, but he said, 'I love rugby! I watch it all the time.'

It was an amazing conversation, because I was just thinking, 'Wow,' and he was just so chilled and nice. And I guess this was the answer to the prayers my fiancée and I had shared on the South Coast. The Arch knew I was a man of God and said, 'Don't worry, I'm going to sort this out for you. Keep on training and playing well and leave it to me; I will resolve this. You will get your citizenship and you'll be able to play for the Springboks.'

As soon as he hung up, my spirits lifted, went through the roof, straight to cloud nine. Now I had someone serious on my side and within a week I got a call from the office of the Minister of Home Affairs, Nkosazana Dlamini-Zuma. I was told to fly up to Pretoria with my documents. So Michelle was literally cut out of the picture

94

and off I went, handed in my stuff, had my fingerprints done, and at the end I was told my passport would be ready in one week!

That was the longest week of my life because, apart from my fiancée and parents, I couldn't tell anyone. I didn't dare breathe a word until I had the passport in my hand. I buried myself in training with the Sharks and a week later I flew back to Pretoria to pick up my passport. Of course, because I had become a South African citizen I now had to surrender my Zimbabwean passport. On my first trip back to Zim there were a few chirps when people saw my South African passport – stuff like, 'He's crossed over to the dark side' – but it was all in good fun and at the end of the day to me it was just a document. It made it easier for me to travel and do my job, but it didn't change who I was and where I was from. The first thing I did was take a picture of the new passport and the next thing I did was to call Regan Hoskins.

On Friday, June 25th, Hoskins released a press statement that read: 'The South African Rugby Union announced on Friday that prop Tendai Mtawarira had been cleared for selection for the Springboks following the granting of South African citizenship.

'Mtawarira was unavailable for selection for the Springboks' first four Tests of 2010 – against Wales, France and Italy (2) – as he was not a holder of a South African passport. The decision to exclude him from selection was taken following advice from the Ministry of Sport reaffirming the government's position that no foreign player can be selected to represent a national team.

'Mtawarira had been actively seeking South African citizenship and has now been granted that right by the Minister for Home Affairs, Dr Nkosazana Dlamini-Zuma.

"'This is very gratifying news indeed and thanks to much hard work that has been going on behind the scenes over the past few months," said Mr Oregan Hoskins, president of the South African Rugby Union. "I'd like to personally thank Minister Dlamini-Zuma for her intervention to assist in this matter. It had long been Beast's desire to become naturalised and he has had to endure some difficult times in recent months. He is now eligible for selection should he fit into the plans of the coach and national selectors.'"

It is difficult to know how the decision was arrived at and until he was interviewed for this book Hoskins had no idea about Tutu's role. It's possible that Tutu called Dlamini-Zuma direct, but it's more likely that he went over her head and straight to the top of the ANC structure.

Sports Minister Stofile left office at the end of October 2010 and, eight months later, took up his post as the ambassador to Germany, a position he fulfilled until his death on August 15th, 2016. His replacement as Sports Minister was Fikile Mbalula, who took a far more benign approach to rugby than his predecessor. But that was all in the future for Beast as he began to come to terms with resuming his international career.

When he heard that everything had been resolved, Peter de Villiers called to tell me how happy he was that I was available, but warned that he wasn't going to pick me for the Tri Nations, but he said he would definitely get me back in the squad for the end-of-year tour.

That wasn't what I wanted to hear, of course, because I was just raring to go. I was a raging bull ready to be unleashed! I remember the hunger I felt having to watch Gurthrö playing my position and I wanted to prove my worth and show people how hungry I was to play in the Bok jersey again.

As for Hoskins, today he ponders whether Beast expected more from the president of Saru than he was able to give. He says: 'I think because he was from Zimbabwe, that Beast assumed I had a lot more power as president of Saru than was actually the case. He didn't understand the political reality in South Africa. From 2006 to 2018 I always felt I had to walk a tightrope. Whenever I had to speak in front of parliament I had to defend rugby and assure them that we were serious about transformation. I always felt I had to mind my Ps and Qs with senior ANC people and that is the saddest part of my time with rugby.

'I believe that the ANC has bullied rugby and my successor as president, Mark Alexander, told me that he has become an ANC member and I get a sense that the relationship has improved because of that. Looking back, maybe if the president of Saru in 2009/10 had been an ANC member we could have stood up to government over Beast. But Butana Komphela and Cedric Frolick and all those guys knew I wasn't an ANC member and at my last meeting at Luthuli House, just before I resigned, it became clear to me that I would never have the backing of the ANC.'

Chapter 10

BEAUTY AND THE BEAST

In 2008 all three Mtawarira brothers were staying at my place in Riverside, just up the road from Kings Park. Brian had come down from Zimbabwe because times were hard at home and he was looking for work, while Ray was accepted at the Sharks Academy. Brian stayed with me for a few weeks and then went down to Cape Town, but it didn't happen for him there, so he came back to Durban and got an opportunity to work at Clifton School in Morningside. He started as an intern and they liked him, so he's still there to this day and now he's a great Maths teacher. He married a girl from Zimbabwe and they have two children. People come up to me at Sharks games and tell me that my brother taught their son and that's really rewarding.

Ray started at Falcon College and then moved to Peterhouse and my sister Lisa went to Peterhouse Girls. I was able to help out with school fees and Lisa is now in Canada studying Biochemistry at the University of Newfoundland. I guess you can say she is the brains of the family and is cruising through her degree. It's rewarding for me to be able to help her in achieving her dreams.

The year 2008 was my breakthrough season, when it was all happening for me; I made my debut for the Boks and then things went to my head. I was excited, I was young and I was living the dream. I started to get up to no good, lost my way a bit, and that's when I discovered that mothers have some kind of sixth sense. They know when something's up with their kids. Some time in June my mum called me and said, 'Tendai, I've been praying. I put my trust in God for your life and the funny thing is that I had a vision while I was in church.'

My mum is a very spiritual woman and tries her best to live a life that is consistent with her faith. She told me that in the vision she saw a girl who goes to our church in Harare and she saw the two of us getting married. She said, 'I really feel that this has come direct from God and I'm not just saying it for the sake of saying it.' On the other end of the line I was just shaking my head and thinking, 'Uh-uh, let's move on ... Change the subject please.' But she wouldn't take no for an answer and said, 'You really have to meet her – I believe that this is your wife.'

The girl in question used to run a Sunday-school class at the Apostolic Faith Mission Church in the centre of Harare and that's where my mum had seen her. Her father, Masimba Makore, had been the main pastor at the church, but he had passed on a few years prior.

Over time, my mum and I had a few more conversations about the vision girl, but each time she came up, I quickly changed the subject or brushed it off and she consistently kept pushing it. Eventually, a few months later, my mum finally gathered enough courage to approach the girl's mom and she told her about her vision. The girl's mom, Margaret, freaked out (as any mother of a 17-year-old would). She told my mum that this was her only daughter and she was very young. I think she doubted the authenticity of the marriage vision. 'I don't even know your son,' she exclaimed. 'How about we start off by meeting your son first, and then we can proceed from there.' It was a fair compromise, I suppose.

My mum still felt strongly, so they agreed to pray together. They prayed and they fasted – and this was all happening behind the scenes while I was busy playing rugby and getting on with my life.

In December 2008, I brought my parents to South Africa for Christmas. It was during this visit that my mother found the opportunity to confront me about 'the girl'. She sat me down and informed me (more like instructed me) to make the first move and contact her.

'How am I going to do that?' I asked. 'Will I have to fly back home?' It was a bit of an exaggerated suggestion as I knew there were other ways of contacting her.

My mother dismissed my concerns by giving me her number. Not only that, she had come armed with pictures of her! I must admit, I liked what I saw. She was light in complexion, wore her hair natural and had it tied in a bun. She had a shy-ish smile that was draped with innocence. No wonder my mum was making such a big fuss about this girl. I could tell that my mum was serious about this as she had never in the past asked me about girls or anything of the sort.

I got my final instructions from her before she left, just before New Year's Eve. 'Call her and have a conversation. If it doesn't

happen, it doesn't happen.' The task was now left with me to call
or not to call.

At this time I was already in a relationship, but I knew in
my heart that that wasn't going to go anywhere. I was young and
I was experimenting and I guess my mum picked up on that and
decided to intervene. Growing up, I had only ever had one girlfriend, because I was always married to my rugby. She was an
athlete at a school in Harare and I went out with her for the last
two years of my time at school. She was a sprinter and we got
along, trained together, but it all came to an end when I went to
the Academy. I wasn't interested in girls back then and my mates
used to worry about me, but that's the way it was; I knew girls
would be a distraction and I didn't want to be distracted.

So it was that on New Year's Day 2009 I took a leap of faith.
I took out the number and the first thing I noticed was that it
was a landline. So now I was freaking out in case someone else
answered and wanted to know why I wanted to speak to her, but
as luck would have it, she answered, 'Hello, this is Kuziva Makore.'
So I introduced myself as Tendai Mtawarira and I could almost
sense her jaw drop at the other end of the line; 'Wow, you actually
called. Your mum told me about you.'

And literally from the first moment we spoke, we hit it off. We
had a natural connection and seemed to agree on most things. She
was hilarious and spoke sarcasm (one of the languages I'm fluent
in), and we laughed a lot! We spoke about how neither of us could
believe how our mothers had got us into this situation, but she
said she wasn't put under any pressure. Her mum just said, 'If he
calls, he calls. Answer the phone. See what happens.'

I called her the next day too and, after a few days, I began to look forward to speaking to her after training. The season started, the Sharks went on tour and we carried on speaking on the phone every day – and it was then that I started to realise something had happened to me. The other Sharks guys noticed and they took an interest. Keegan Daniel even found out that her full name was Kuzivakwashe. The fact of the matter was that, after three months, I had fallen in love over the phone. I couldn't wait to see her.

At the time, I couldn't fly to Harare because we were too busy, but on April 1st my mum flew to South Africa with Kuziva. We were playing the Hurricanes that Saturday and I was at training, so I couldn't meet them at the airport. I did, though, take a change of clothes with me to training and when the moment came I was completely overdressed. I generally live in shorts and a T-shirt, but I was wearing the only formal suit I owned, along with a white collared shirt and my prized lace-up black shoes. I drove home to meet her at my place in Riverside. Fortunately for me, she was also overdressed. To see her in the flesh after only ever seeing photos was amazing; I was so emotional, but eventually I calmed down and asked her if she was hungry. I think my mum had already explained to her how important food was in my life, so off we went for an early supper to a restaurant around the corner.

Kuziva – Ku, to her friends – remembers her first meeting with Beast's mother. 'Bertha was straight to the point. She said, "I really like you and I think you should meet my son." And I had the biggest eyes ever. To be honest, it came in one ear and out the other, but she gave me Tendai's number and she asked if she could give my number to him and, just to get her to shut up, I said okay. Well, obviously I didn't call him and for about six months he didn't call me and every Sunday I had to meet his mum in church and she would say, "Did he call?" and I would say, "No." Then one day she came with a Sharks magazine and Tendai was on the cover and she was so proud of her son. But I wasn't sporty and although I knew what rugby was, I really wasn't interested in it.

'On New Year's Day he finally called, and when he said "Hello" in that deep voice he got me. I tried to act nonchalant, but he got me and we spoke for hours and then he asked if he could call me again that night. So I said okay and that was the beginning. Then we spoke every day for three months and eventually he suggested I come to South Africa to see him and I had to explain that I would have to sell the idea to my mother. Well, mum said, "No. If he wants to see you he should come here." So it took a lot of negotiations, but eventually, with Bertha as my chaperone, I was allowed to go.

'I got on a plane for the first time in my life. We arrived on the Friday and he was off at captain's run and so I met his brother, Ray, before I met him. When he did come home he was very overdressed, but he was such a gentleman. I met him on the Friday and on the Saturday Bertha and I went to the Sharks game and she's introducing me as Tendai's girlfriend to anyone who will listen. After the game we went to the area where the Sharks guys park their cars and here comes Keegan Daniel saying, "Kuziva Makore, Kuziva Makore, I've heard way too much about you. I feel like I know you."

'It made me feel good that Tendai had been telling people about me because, I won't lie, after I saw the article in the Sharks magazine I was thinking he must be really famous and girls must be throwing *themselves at him, so why would he be interested in poor old me? And even though we had built a relationship on the phone I was still thinking that maybe he was just doing this to get his mother off his back, so he could say, "I've met her and I didn't like her. Now go away." But when Keegan said those things, I thought, 'That's nice, maybe he's not wasting my time after all."*

'The next day in a quiet moment he said, "What would you say if I proposed to you?" and I was really caught off guard. Unbeknown to me, he went and called my mum the next day and she nearly had an accident. She spoke to him and said, "Don't be rushing anything. Nobody's chasing you. You need to make sure this is love and not infatuation."

'He also told his mum and on the Wednesday she said to me, "We need to get you a dress – we're going out to dinner and you'll be meeting the Sharks players so you need to look smart." And I told her I had a dress, but she was very insistent, so off we went and at every shop we went to I would try something on and she would say, "It's very nice, but it's not what this occasion calls for." And I was so naïve I had no idea what occasion she was talking about. So we got the dress and then she said we need shoes and to get your hair done, and, and, and ...'

Everything was just perfect. We got on really well and the week flew by; on the Saturday we beat the Hurricanes and by Sunday I knew I wanted to marry this girl. I took her to the Midlands for a picnic and in the car we were listening to music. One song in particular made an impression on us; it was Tracy Chapman singing 'I Am Yours'.

I knew this was the one, so now I needed a ring. At the time the Sharks' physio was Ruan Fourie who, in his spare time, was a diamond dealer. He organised a nice rock for me and things started falling into place. There wasn't time to set the stone in a ring, but I figured we could do that later. The Sharks were playing in Bloemfontein against the Cheetahs the next Saturday, but I was rested, maybe because we had won seven out of eight games in Super Rugby and Plum thought I needed a break.

Before I could go any further I had to call Kuziva's mum and ask permission to marry her daughter. I said, 'You probably need to sit down,' and she said, 'I am sitting down, I'm driving in the car.' So I told her that I was really grateful that she had allowed Kuziva to come and meet me, that we had had an amazing time and that she was definitely the one for me and I wanted to propose to her. Well, she almost crashed! She had to pull over to the side of the road, and she went, 'Whoa, whoa, whoa! What are you saying, Tendai? Don't you think it's a bit too soon? Are you sure? You've just met her.'

And I said, 'I know. My heart is telling me.'

Eventually she calmed down and said, 'Okay. I give you my blessing.'

It was Easter weekend and on Good Friday I went to a restaurant near my place and spoke to the manager. I explained that I wanted to make it a special night for my fiancée-to-be and we already had a special song that I wanted him to play at the right time. I arranged a special meal as well: steak followed by cheesecake, with champagne. Ku loves pudding and I do too – I'm a sucker for chocolate cake, but I can't go near it most of the time, so in the off season I go crazy!

At first I thought it would be best if it was just the two of us, but then I thought, 'No, let's make it a party.' So I invited one of my really good friends from church, Kudzai and her husband Israel, my mum of course, and Ray, who was living with me anyway.

Ku takes up the story: 'Well, Friday comes and everyone in the house is dressed up and Ray is filming people with his camcorder and I still have no idea what's going on. We get to the restaurant and I'm expecting a 40-seater table because I had been lied to that it was for the rugby boys. Meanwhile, there's just six of us. Then this Tracy Chapman song comes on and he gets down on one knee. I have no idea what he said, because my ears had started ringing and I was in such shock, but fortunately I knew my answer, which was, "Yes." So he dropped the diamond in my hand and told me I must design a ring to go around it.'

Ku's ears may have been ringing, but fortunately, Tendai remembers what he said.

I told her that she had changed my life, that I had fallen in love and wanted to spend the rest of my life with her. My heart was racing as I pulled out the diamond and she was astonished, but she said yes and everyone in the restaurant went nuts.

It was a great night, but eventually Ku had to return to Zimbabwe, to go back to school, and I had to get back to the Sharks. She was in her final year and writing A Levels and I didn't want to distract her too much, but I went to visit her in Zim whenever I could. She duly finished school and decided that she wanted to study marketing, so in the New Year she came to South Africa, stayed with my friend Kudzai, and registered at Varsity College in Pietermaritzburg. The move coincided with the Department of Sport trying to kick me out of the Springboks and she became my pillar of strength. She was by my side through all the hard times.

I received my South African passport at the end of June 2010 and the Boks were already in camp, because the first game was against the All Blacks in Auckland on July 10th. Peter de Villiers decided it was too soon to call me into the squad, so I played Currie Cup for the Sharks and, as it turned out, we won for the second time in three years. But more importantly, it was time for me to get married, so we set the date as Sunday, September 12th. I had to ask Plum for time off and he said, 'It's fine, but don't think you're going on honeymoon just yet!' But it worked out well nevertheless; the Sharks had a Friday-night game in Witbank where they beat the Pumas 30–14 and the Tri Nations had finished the previous weekend, so all my mates were available for the wedding. Jannie and Bismarck were there, Odwa Ndungane, Lwazi Mvovo, Regan Hoskins, Paul Davies, Peter de Villiers, Aaron Denenga, and my best man was Chiliboy Ralepelle.

The venue was Crowhurst Manor in Kloof, which had its own chapel, so we could do everything on site. One of the ideas we came up with to make it extravagant was to build a walkway across the swimming pool, which the wedding party would walk across on the way to the altar. The night before the wedding we were rehearsing and everything was looking magnificent. The guy who built the walkway across the pool said, 'I know you guys are big rugby boys, but I can tell you that this thing is 100% safe. I'm going to show you how strong it is,' and with that he walked into the middle, jumped in the air and crashed straight through it into the pool below!

Ku was watching all of this and she was beside herself. The wedding was the next day and here was the builder wringing wet. He, of course, apologised profusely and assured us that everything would be all right on the day. It'd taken him a week to install this thing and now he had to work right through the night to get it right. He got his hands on some steel, because he had to make it super strong as nobody trusted him after the accident. You can imagine the stress, Ku thinking that if somebody had to fall in the pool this wedding was going to be a joke. And on the day, we finally walked across, and Jannie and Bizzy were standing at the side of the pool chirping loudly, but thankfully it worked and nothing broke. The day was just perfect and I got very emotional when I saw Ku walk down the aisle.

The perfect wedding present arrived six weeks later when we won the Currie Cup, beating Western Province in the final at Kings Park. Then I got back into the Bok side and Ku came with me on tour to Europe. Peter de Villiers welcomed me back into the side – 'We've missed you,' he said – and I wanted to prove to him that I was ready to be first choice again. He backed me and I started in all the Tests. We beat Ireland 23–21, then Wales 29–25, but came unstuck against Scotland in dreadful weather condi-tions in Edinburgh. It was an ugly day and we just made too many errors.

As it turns out, Scotland's 21–17 victory robbed the Boks of their best chance to clinch a Grand Slam in 50 years. Avril Malan's tourists of 1960–61 remain the last Boks to beat all four home

unions in Britain. Just one week earlier, Scotland had been humili-
ated 49–3 by the All Blacks and the Murrayfield Test had long been
regarded as a banker win for the Boks. But the week prior to the
game proved a traumatic one for the visitors when Beast's best man,
Chiliboy Ralepelle, and Bulls wing Bjorn Basson were sent home
after failing a drugs test. Following the match against Ireland, the
pair tested positive for the banned stimulant methylhexaneamine,
and were banned from all rugby until the results of their B-samples
were available. The Bok management team responded by suspend-
ing the use of dietary supplements by the squad, sending a range of
products to be tested in order to ascertain the source of the banned
stimulant.

This was quite a scary time, because everyone knew it could
easily have been any one of them. Chili and Bjorn had to leave
camp immediately and I remember Chili going in front of the
team to say goodbye. He's a really strong character and I'm sure
he was hurting inside and scared for the future, but he portrayed
that positive mindset, said he would get over it and wished the
team well. It was quite an emotional send-off and it was only at
the end that he broke down. We all gathered round and tried to
give him strength. Bjorn wasn't as strong – he couldn't even face
the team. He was hurting for something he felt wasn't his fault and
now he had to go home. He couldn't even speak.

To make matters worse for the team, Bryan Habana broke his
hand while training in Edinburgh, although the positive spin-off was
that one of Beast's wedding guests, Lwazi Mvovo, got to make his
Test debut against Scotland.

The weather did the Boks no favours, but even so, they had enough chances to win. Morné and Frans Steyn each missed early shots at goal that seemed insignificant at the time but loomed large as the Scots built up a 21–12 lead. Beast's Sharks colleague, Willem Alberts, scored a try in the 71st minute to narrow the gap to four points, but no further score was forthcoming. The team bounced back the following week with a convincing 21–11 win against England to finish the tour on a high note.

For the newlyweds something far more significant happened next.

We went on honeymoon! Ku had been on tour with us, but most of the time she was with my family in a house I had rented in London. Finally, with rugby behind us, we were able to let our hair down and we started a fantastic trip in Paris. From there we went to Biarritz and then to the Pyrenees, on into Spain to San Sebastián and finished up in Barcelona. We had the time of our lives and Ku, who was just 19, got to realise her dream of travelling the world.

Chapter 11

DOCTOR, I'M IN TROUBLE

Early in the 2010 Super Rugby season, Beast got the biggest scare of his rugby career. He was diagnosed with a heart condition that could have been fatal if not properly treated.

In April 2010 we had been for a team coffee at Kings Park. There was a coffee place around the corner so this was something we did every second day. But this particular day I finished my coffee and I suddenly felt my heart racing, beating out of my chest. I spend my life doing cardiovascular exercise and I knew how a raised heart rate felt, but this was something completely different. So I jumped in my car and went straight to see the Sharks team doctor, Craig Roberts; he took one listen and sent me off to a specialist.

Dr Dirk Pretorius is a cardiologist who practises in Durban. He told me that my heart was out of synchronisation and asked when it had started. I explained that this was the first time and that all I could think was that the coffee might have had an effect. He agreed that sometimes coffee can trigger these reactions, but the first thing we had to do was get my heart back in synch. So off we went to hospital and by now I was starting to panic. I said, 'I have a big game on the weekend,' and he reassured me that he would sort it out.

They had to do a couple of assessment tests and by the time they knocked me out with a general anaesthetic and applied a defibrillator, my heart had been racing for about two hours. Using a defibrillator is a little like jump-starting a car. They attach wires to your chest and shock you with them.

When I came round, they told me that my heart was now beating normally and that the next step was to sort it out so that it wouldn't happen again. Obviously, the first thing I wanted to know was whether I could still play rugby and they reassured me that it shouldn't affect my career, but you wouldn't want it to happen too often. Dr Pretorius mentioned a specialist in Cape Town, one of the best in the world at the cardiac-ablation operation that corrects irregular heart rhythm; cardiac arrhythmia is what I had. I was told that if it happened again then this was the guy to contact.

And, sure enough, a couple of weeks later we were playing the Blues in a Super Rugby game at Kings Park and it happened during the game. I was just running around in general play, about an hour into the game, and suddenly I felt it and I thought, 'I know this feeling.' I played on for a few minutes, but eventually I had to come off and told Craig Roberts what was happening. He had me rushed to hospital and they had to jump-start me again with the defibrillator. The procedure worked, but now I had to think long-term, so I made contact with the surgeon in Cape Town. It was decided that I would get the season out of the way and then go see him in December.

Dr Faizel Lorgat is an interventional cardiologist based at the Netcare Christiaan Barnard Memorial Hospital in Cape Town. Faizel is the brother of Haroon Lorgat, the former chief executive of both Cricket South Africa and the International Cricket Council. When he saw Beast for the first time in December 2010, Dr Lorgat had just 15 months' experience of the operation required, but by January 2016 he had performed more than a thousand of the procedures and is now regarded as a world authority. Appropriately, given that it is named in honour of Dr Christiaan Barnard, the surgeon who changed the world with his heart transplant technique, the Cape Town facility where Dr Lorgat works was the first in the southern hemisphere to perform this heart operation with its cutting-edge technology.

Atrial fibrillation is the most common cause of cardioembolic stroke. To explain it better, consider the role of the heart in circulating blood throughout the body to distribute oxygen and essential nutrients. Oxygenated blood is collected from the lungs and pumped via the left atrium at the top of the heart into the left ventricle just below it, then into the aorta and out into the rest of the body. The blood is then pumped through the right atrium into the right ventricle and back to the lungs via the pulmonary artery. This circular process is controlled by a series of coordinated electrical impulses. However, if for some reason the timing of these electrical pulses is thrown out, the walls of the atria can vibrate rapidly. This is called fibrillation, the racing heart effect referred to by Beast, and the way to stop it is, logically enough, with a defibrillator.

But defibrillation deals with the symptoms, not the cause. The operation used by Dr Lorgat employs a robotic catheter system fitted with a radio-frequency device, which works like a laser to cauterise or ablate overactive or damaged electrical pathways that cause electrical disturbances in the heart. This enables the heart's rhythm to return to normal, reducing the need for other treatments such as pacemakers and medication. Dr Lorgat says that the system allows 'short circuits' in the heart to be destroyed with a heated catheter tip. Nick Mallett, the former Springbok coach, who recently underwent the operation, describes the effect produced as, 'Like burning a firebreak around the heart'.

When I got back from my honeymoon I went to see Dr Pretorius and he referred me to Dr Lorgat in Cape Town. I was told if I had the operation I could do no physical activity for a month. That meant I would only be able to join pre-season training very late, but Plum said, 'Go sort yourself out,' and it wasn't a problem from a Sharks perspective. Dr Lorgat told me not to worry, that he'd done this many times and the whole operation lasted about four hours. They put a catheter through my groin all the way to my heart and then burnt away the nerve endings that were causing the problem.

I spent two days recuperating in hospital. Although I was feeling disorientated and my groin was really sore, I had prayed and had faith that I was in good hands, so I was confident that the healing process would be a smooth one. Ku was an inspiration as well, urging me to leave it all in God's hands.

Back home, it was hard for me to sit and do nothing, but

it was an opportunity to recover from a few other niggles that you pick up along the way as a professional rugby player. By then we had moved into our new house in La Lucia, and there were a few Sharks players who were now my neighbours. Bismarck and Jannie shared a house down the road, and Keegan Daniel and Craig Burden were also nearby, so I had support from people who knew how I was feeling. Obviously there was a lot of negativity from people who didn't really know what was wrong with me, claiming I wouldn't be as strong or as fast as I had been before, but I learned to put that kind of talk to one side.

By the end of January 2011, I was able to get back into light training but then there was a flare-up during the Super Rugby season. I had to get defibrillated again and Dr Pretorius suggested I get a second operation. Apparently, this wasn't unusual and I was told not to worry, but this was a World Cup year and the last thing I wanted to do was to miss that. So I played on and it was decided that I could have the operation at the end of the season, just as I'd had it the previous year. So I went to see Dr Lorgat again and all went well and that was the end of that. Or so I thought.

But then, on the end-of-year tour with the Springboks in 2012, it happened again. The day before the Test against Ireland in Dublin I went out for dinner with a couple of the boys. My heart suddenly started racing again and I knew immediately what it was. I ran to Craig Roberts and cried on his shoulder. Craig had been the Sharks doctor when this had happened the first time, so he knew my history. He took me to the nearest hospital and explained the issue to them. They put me under, defibrillated me and when I came round I was informed I would be watching the

Test match on television from a hospital bed. The thing was, I knew that once I had been defibrillated everything would be fine, but they insisted on keeping me in for observation. I flew from Dublin to Edinburgh on the Sunday, fully expecting to be in contention for a spot in the team to play Scotland, but Craig had called Dr Pretorius and he had said I should come home to see him and arrange a third trip to Dr Lorgat.

I remember going back to my room and just losing it, weeping on my own and wondering why on earth it was happening again. Up until that point I had faith in the advice the doctors were giving me, but now I was really scared. I caught the next flight back to South Africa and headed off to have more tests with Dr Pretorius. He tried to pick me up, saying that sometimes it takes three attempts to fix the problem and that I shouldn't stress, that I would get back soon enough and play many more games. But I was a little sceptical and was scared to even tell my parents, because they were likely to tell me enough is enough, especially my old man.

Every time any of these occurrences had taken place I had had to have tests and there was never a hint of scandal. My record was clean, I'd never taken pills and had even steered clear of supplements. I would drink stuff like Powerade and caffeine drinks before a game, but when Dr Pretorius told me that caffeine had probably caused my first two episodes in 2010, I cut those out as well.

So, after my consultation with Dr Pretorius, off I went to see Dr Lorgat for the third time. I knew what to expect, but this time I wasn't as sure. By now I was uncertain about my future in rugby and this time I was really on my own because Ku had to stay in Durban to study for an exam. As a result, I wasn't as positive as I had been the two previous occasions and had to spend longer recovering from the operation. It seemed to me that each time I did this, things got slower and I had to work harder to start to feel normal again.

Back home, I moped around for a few weeks, wondering whether I had the strength to put myself through all of this again, but one day I had one of those lightbulb moments and realised that the best was yet to come. I felt really strongly about it and simply decided to change my whole mindset. I realised that there were people out there who were going through a lot worse than I was and that it was time to fight. Ku was always the voice of positivity around me and she fed me the right stuff, by which I mean not just food, but advice. There was media talk that I wasn't going to come back from this, but I didn't let that get to me. The thing was that it had never affected my game, never slowed me down.

It's been seven years since then and I've never had a recurrence.

Today I get people contacting me on social media asking for advice. They have the same problem, or are having the same procedure and want to know my experiences and how I got rid of it. Just last year I got a phone call from Plum's wife, Lara, asking who I went to see and what advice I could give because apparently it's happened to Plum a couple of times. I try to encourage people, tell them that the condition is not life threatening – because that's the first thing anybody thinks when it happens to them. I guess I have become an ambassador for Dr Lorgart's work because I give him a lot of credit, which he deserves.

117

Chapter 12

DEFENDING THE CUP

Right at the start of the 2011 Super Rugby season John Plumtree found himself in a very difficult situation. Bismarck was playing the best rugby of his life, but John Smit was the team captain. Plum had to figure out how to manage the two. It became pretty difficult for him to start John every week, because Bizzy was just the best. Because John needed game time, there were heated arguments between him and Plum. It was a World Cup year and John obviously wanted to retain the Springbok captaincy, which he couldn't do if he didn't play. He was under a lot of pressure and I think Bizzy revelled in the circumstances, because he knew John had to play out of his skin from week to week.

The experiment of playing John Smit at tighthead had come to an end two years prior and, in any case, Jannie du Plessis was there now and I was at loosehead. John didn't play in the first game of the season against the Cheetahs, but he came off the bench at hooker in the next game against the Blues and then we went on tour to Australia. We beat the Force in Perth and John

118

came off the bench to replace Jannie at tighthead. The following week, in Melbourne, Plum started John and benched Jannie, but we won and that made it four wins from four games.

We then flew on to New Zealand and I think that at some stage John and Plum had a sit-down. They decided that John was now going to play loosehead, so Plum came to me before one of the training sessions and said, 'Beast, you're young, you've got a lot of years left in you, so you can afford to take a break. What I'm gonna do is start John at loosehead and you can pick up again later.'

I didn't say anything to Plum then, but in my head I thought, 'What's this crap?' Obviously Plum was under pressure to make a plan so I was now being benched. It motivated me to work harder, though, because now I had a point to prove. I was upset and angry, but I was young and couldn't take Plum on. Anyway, we lost 15–9 to the Chiefs in Hamilton and the following week we had to play the Crusaders in London.

The Crusaders were forced onto the road in the 2011 Super Rugby season. On Tuesday, February 22nd, at 12.51pm local time, New Zealand's South Island was struck by an earthquake measuring 6.3 on the Richter scale. The epicentre was just 10 kilometres south of Christchurch, New Zealand's third-most populous city; 185 people were killed and a number of buildings were reduced to rubble.

A state of emergency was declared and, as a mark of respect, the Crusaders' match against the Hurricanes, due to be played on the Saturday, was scrapped. The Crusaders subsequently played most of their home games in Nelson, but in a move aimed at popularising

*Super Rugby beyond the southern hemisphere, it was decided that
they would host the Sharks at Twickenham, the London headquar-
ters of the English Rugby Football Union (RFU).*

Originally Plum had told me that I would be starting against
the Crusaders, but when in London he came to me and said that
he had decided to start with John at loosehead. I was devastated
– it was a big game, in London, against the Crusaders, and I had
been relishing the prospect. When Plum told me, I was really
angry, ready to punch the wall because I couldn't believe he was
going to take that stance.

So John started the game and the Crusaders' All Black front
row just hammered us. Owen Franks was at tighthead, Corey
Flynn was hooker and Wyatt Crockett was the loosehead. They
had obviously targeted our scrum from the moment they heard
John was going to be at loosehead and they smashed us up front,
with Franks having an absolute field day. Pretty soon Plum realised he had to make a change and I came on with about half an
hour left in the game.

I was angry and I just let everything out. I took it out on
the Crusaders – I think I even hit someone; it might have been
Richie McCaw. I was driven by anger and played the game of my
life. I remember seeing blood and the feeling that I had to show
Plum that my jersey belongs to me. Well, he noticed all right, but it
didn't change his mind because he brought John off the bench to
replace me against the Stormers and started him against the Lions
in the next game. But he couldn't even face me, didn't even want to
look me in the eye, because he knew it was wrong.

In a way, that decision changed my relationship with John

and caused some friction.

Towards the end of the Super Rugby season we played the Bulls at Loftus and Bizzy put in an outstanding, man-of-the-match performance. It was a really tight game that we ended up winning 26–23, and Plum obviously felt he couldn't make a change. John ended up playing about four minutes as a replacement for Bizzy. After the game there was a heated exchange between John and Plum, because John hadn't had as much game time as he would have wanted.

At the same time, though, whether or not he was the best player in whatever position for which he was picked, the fact remains that John was a great leader. He was a charismatic talker who could really get the guys going, especially when times were tough on the field, because that's when he would rise up. At that time, the Springboks had a really strong leadership team. John was tight with Victor, Fourie and Schalk – they had been through a lot together. But, whereas I don't think anyone seriously thought there were better players than the other three, there was definitely a target on John's back. Everyone knew that Bizzy should have been starting and had more influence on the field. So I guess you could argue that there was some underlying stuff that hadn't been dealt with by the time the World Cup came around. We just got on with it, but we knew that John was not playing in his prime position and it didn't make a lot of sense because that just weakened the team.

In 2011 the Boks sent a B side on tour to Australia and New Zealand, in order to protect the players who would form the core of the side

121

*that would go to the World Cup. Players such as Deon Stegmann,
Charl McLeod and Alistair Hargreaves were capped in these games,
both of which ended in heavy defeat for the tourists. Significantly,
however, John Smit remained captain and continued to pick up time
at loosehead prop in the second half of each game when Chiliboy
Ralepelle came off the bench to play at hooker.*

*Beast was one of the players who stayed at home, but he did
take the field against Australia at Kings Park on August 13th along
with the rest of the 'A Team'. The result was not what the management team was hoping for, however, as the Boks went down 14–9. The
home side was leading 6–0 at the break, but the Wallabies scored
twice in the first 10 minutes after the resumption to take an 8–6 lead.
Crucially, the decision was made to replace Jannie du Plessis with
half an hour to go. His brother, Bismarck, went to hooker and, with
no tighthead cover on the bench, Smit was moved across. The Bok
scrum 'found itself in reverse' according to* SA Rugby Annual, *and
that set the tone for the rest of the match.*

*Smit and Beast were benched for the final game of the Tri
Nations season and coach Peter de Villiers handed the captaincy to
Victor Matfield. The All Blacks had also decided to send a weakened side on tour and that worked in the Boks' favour, as the boot
of Morné Steyn kicked them to an 18–5 win in Port Elizabeth. The
Boks now went into camp to prepare to defend their World Cup title
in New Zealand.*

Before departing for New Zealand, we had a team-building
session in the Kruger Park. We were in tents in the middle of
nowhere, with lions roaming around just outside, so it was quite
scary. India had won the Cricket World Cup earlier that year and

their coach was the South African, Gary Kirsten. He came and spoke to us around the bonfire and offered some of the secrets of his team's success. The following day we were given another inspiring talk, this time by 'the Human Polar Bear', Lewis Pugh. He spoke for an hour about the way he lives his life and that made a lasting impression on me. That night we flew off to my first World Cup. I was positive, excited, ready and hungry.

For the first two matches of the World Cup we were based in Wellington. The first game against Wales was really tough and physical. Wales played out of their skins and we did well to win. With 25 minutes to go, John and I were replaced by Bizzy and Gurthrö. The next game, against Fiji, Gurthrö started and I was on the bench, but I came on for the last 15 minutes and scored a try. It was quite a special day because both the loosehead props scored! Mine was in the 70th minute; Frans Steyn made a great break down the middle and I was there lurking in support. I thought that when he was tackled he would just reach out and score, but instead he offloaded to me and I grabbed it, put my head down and got over the line. It was only the second try I had scored for the Boks, the first since the one against Italy three years previously, and obviously it was special because it was in the World Cup.

Gurthrö started against Namibia and we won 87–0, but I was back in the starting team for the last pool match against Samoa at North Harbour Stadium in Auckland. It was a game of big hits from the Samoans, but we played smartly, hurting them at set-piece time. It was a sound win, but my body was battered and bruised afterwards, having scrummed against Census Johnston, a big guy of almost 140 kilograms. The forwards had a good day at the office – and stuck to the plan, kept our discipline. Samoa, on the other hand, tend to get a little too wild and to give away penalties from cheap shots.

The Boks had the benefit of a stiff wind behind them in the first half and were able to build up a 13–0 lead that was ultimately too much for Samoa, who nevertheless won the second half 5–0 thanks to a try by George Stowers. Bryan Habana's ninth-minute try (his fortieth in Test rugby) suggested a far more straightforward win than was ultimately the case. As Beast recalls, the Boks stuck to their structures and with Matfield stealing opposition ball at the lineouts and Heinrich Brüssow doing likewise at the rucks, the Samoans were forced to run the scraps of possession that came their way.

Significantly, the team was captained by Matfield and when Smit came off the bench in the 69th minute he lasted just two minutes before being yellow carded for a deliberate slap-down of the ball. Steenkamp replaced Beast for the last 20 minutes and with pool play now at an end, the management team had nine days to mull over what team to select for the quarterfinal against Australia in Wellington. One important decision was out of their hands, however, and that was the appointment of the match officials. Bryce Lawrence of New Zealand had been one of the touch judges who turned a blind eye to the Bulls' indiscretions in the desperate final seconds of the 2007 Super Rugby final. Now he would be the referee in Wellington.

On the Tuesday I was told that I was not going to be playing in the quarterfinal. Originally, Peter had told me that he wanted to start Gurthrö and that I would be on the bench. He felt that Gurthrö was doing really well and that I was making an impact off the bench, but on the Tuesday Jannie du Plessis was not feeling well and that upset Peter's plan, which was for John to go to tight-head when Jannie came off and that I replace Gurthrö. But with Jannie off, Peter was unsure and because it was such a big Test match he felt he needed an experienced tighthead on the bench, so CJ van der Linde got the nod.

Peter realised how upset I was, but assured me that I would be back for the semi-final, but then – guess what – we didn't make the semi-final. I couldn't believe it when Peter broke the news; I was young and eager and I just wanted to play. I was gutted and it was hard to get up for training, but eventually I came to terms with the situation and did my utmost to give my best for the team that was playing. In the end, of course, CJ stayed on the bench and wasn't used.

On the day of the game, as a non-playing member of the squad, I was dressed in my Springbok number-ones and sat next to Chiliboy in the stands. It was really awkward walking up those stairs to sit right at the top and all the way people were saying, 'Why you not playing, Beast?' They were in my face and I really didn't enjoy it. Then they started to get abusive, saying, 'You guys are gonna lose.'

We were sitting among the Aussie supporters and I wondered who would organise something like that? I didn't understand why the organisers would seat players in the stands instead of down behind the team. It was unbearable because people were hurling abuse and you weren't allowed to retaliate. Anyway, we watched the game from there and I thought we played really well; we had a really good first half, and Pat Lambie scored a try that was turned down by the ref.

And thereby hangs a tale. In the days following the game, referee Bryce Lawrence came in for a pasting in the media for a host of controversial decisions. In the UK's Daily Telegraph, *Mark Reason wrote, 'Despite all the fantastic players on the pitch, the match became a farce because Lawrence had absolutely no control over the breakdown. Players were diving in on all sides. It became a free-for-all. What could have been a great game of rugby turned into a mess, because Lawrence did not rule the breakdown.' Even John Smit, who would usually shun controversy, was angered enough to say, 'His refereeing of the breakdown was disgraceful. He let David Pocock get away with murder. Little wonder he won the Man of the Match award.'*

In the hurly-burly of post-match analysis, so much attention was focused on Lawrence's refereeing at the breakdown that few recalled the most crucial error of all. It was the moment in the 45th minute of the game when Pat Lambie's try was overturned by the referee, who claimed the final pass from Jean de Villiers had been forward.

De Villiers says, 'It was the winning try by Pat, and my pass wasn't forward. When you play the game, sometimes you make a pass and then you look up to the ref with that guilty look, knowing that it might have been forward. In that instance, I didn't even think about it. That was the funny thing and when I heard about Pat's retirement I sent him a message saying, "I still remember your winning try against Australia in the quarterfinals."' Millions watching on television and those crammed into the ground – known as 'The Cake Tin' in Wellington – watched the defending champions crash out as a direct result of incompetent officiating. Beast says he could see it clearly from his place in the top tier.

I felt that Bryce Lawrence's body language throughout the game was a dead giveaway, that he was not going to let us win. He was one-sided and the calls that went against us weren't even 50/50. Heinrich Brüssow went off injured after 20 minutes and after that David Pocock had a huge impact on the game. He stole a lot of ball and he was very effective at the breakdown. He caused havoc and that meant we couldn't get momentum and the game slowly slipped out of our hands. I remember thinking, 'If only I could have played a few minutes; if only I had been allowed to make an impact, maybe just maybe the result could have been different.' I was angry and I couldn't believe that the World Cup had ended, but Chili reminded me that we were young, that there would be other World Cups and the best was yet to come.

After the game we had a team meeting to say goodbye to each other. It was very emotional and there were tears, and some great words from the senior guys who were leaving, guys like John Smit, Fourie du Preez, Victor Matfield and Danie Rossouw. They were handing over to the next generation of Springboks and my feeling was that this was just the beginning, that it was time for me to step up and become more of a leader, because I was hungry to play for the Boks. If that was to happen I would have to prove myself to the new Springbok coach, because the World Cup quarterfinal was Peter de Villiers's last game in charge.

Peter copped a lot of flak during his four years in charge

of the Boks, but he was wise enough as coach to let the players express themselves and he did a good job of motivating and managing the squad. He knew there was nothing he could teach Victor about the lineout, but Victor got help from assistant coach Gary Gold, who did a lot of research. But even there, Gary would pass on information but leave it to Victor to make the final decisions with John Smit.

The backline was more democratic, but Jean de Villiers played a massive role and, from a defensive perspective, Jaque Fourie was in charge. Jaque was pretty vocal and said a lot of powerful things, not just to the backs but to the whole team. For my part, it was still like playing with your heroes, the guys you looked up to. I was constantly pinching myself that I was playing in the same team as Schalk Burger, Bryan Habana and those guys, but my philosophy was that I wanted to learn as much as I could while it lasted. I would spend a lot of time listening and one guy who was always happy to talk to me was Bryan. I would ask him how he managed to stay at the top of his game and I was ready to receive anything he was able to pass down to me. Bakkies was also very open.

Most of the time, though, it was hard to approach those guys. Players such as Fourie du Preez, Schalk and Victor shared a kind of brotherhood that you just couldn't crack. They were a tight group and it was intimidating for a youngster to have, for instance, a conversation with Victor. You felt like you knew nothing. I played with Schalk for my first four seasons and had no more than a handful of conversations with him in all that time, mostly to say hello in the morning.

And it wasn't just me. I think Peter de Villiers also felt a bit of an outsider. He had been a great coach of the Junior Springboks, but I think at the higher level he was probably fortunate that he was handed a really good squad of players. His methods and approach didn't always work with the Springboks. And some of the media didn't like Peter and thought he was something of a clown, and there's no doubt he was fortunate that he was in charge of a team that could take charge of its own course. Peter didn't do much; most of the work was done by the players and, of course, Gary and Dick were very influential. But at the end of the day, Peter was the coach who first picked me for the Springboks and he stood by me through all the trouble with the Minister of Sport, so I'm really grateful to him.

Chapter 13

BROKEN BONES AND TIME ZONES

I was pretty excited at the beginning of 2012 when I heard that Heyneke Meyer was to be the new Springbok coach. He had a lot of success with the Bulls, and Chili – who had played under Heyneke for the Bulls – told me he was a good, principled man. The first time I got to meet him was when he came to the Sharks during the 2012 Super Rugby season. He was doing the rounds of all the franchises. The Sharks had a poor start to the season – we had a really good squad that just wasn't producing. Plum had to work really hard to turn things around, but eventually the team started to gel.

Because I broke my ankle in pre-season training, I missed the first nine games of the season. To get us fit at training, Plum enjoyed playing 10s. It was about a week and a half ahead of the first game of the season, I got the ball from Bismarck, was having a nice run down the field and I didn't see Keegan, who came from the side and blindsided me. He hit me and, simultaneously, my foot got caught, twisting in a funny way, and my ankle went: broken.

Lying on the field waiting for the medical staff, I was thinking, 'It's all going to be okay, maybe it's just a sprain,' but as soon as I went for the scan I could clearly see the break in the tibia. Keegan was distraught, but rugby is a contact sport and these things happen. It was the first time in my life I had ever broken a bone and it was a real setback; I was in good condition and ready for the season, but I used the opportunity to spend quality time with the family. I went for the operation and knew I would be out for a few months, so I just had to sit on the sidelines.

It took six to eight weeks before I was walking properly and it was a really frustrating time for me because the team wasn't doing well. All I wanted to do was come back and make a difference, because I could tell that the team's morale wasn't great. My rehab went well and the injury healed quicker than anyone was expecting. After two months I was able to start jogging and from there it was a case of increasing the pace and building the confidence to be able to change direction.

I made my comeback for the Vodacom Cup side – the KwaZulu-Natal Wildebeest – against the Eastern Province Kings on April 21st. The game was at Kings Park and we were the curtain raiser to the Sharks playing the Chiefs. The Wildebeest won, but the Sharks lost 18–12, which meant that they had won four and lost five in their first nine games. The Sharks had a bye the following week, which gave me another chance to work on my match fitness. The Wildebeest travelled down to Stellenbosch and we beat the Pampas XV, the team from Argentina.

Everything went fine, so the week after the bye Plum brought me back into the Sharks team for the game against the Highlanders at Kings Park. I'm sure it's just a coincidence, but from the moment I got back into the side the Sharks started winning again – in fact, we won eight of the next nine games and qualified for the finals.

My first match back was a good one for Pat Lambie, who scored all our points with a try, conversion and seven penalties, driving us home to a 28–16 win. We all enjoyed playing with Pat and he made a lasting impression at the Sharks. It was the way he handled himself that stood out; he was the ultimate professional who always worked very hard and never let the success get to his head. He stayed humble and treated everyone around him with respect, and by that I mean not just the guys in the team, but everybody. From a rugby point of view, he was the ultimate gentleman. He was a great leader as well, one who managed to stay calm and make the right decisions under pressure, and those qualities were already there even as a very young man making his way at the Sharks.

Pat never backed away from contact. He made big hits and carried the ball hard to the line and I remember in particular the way he dumped Schalk Burger with a huge handoff on his way to score in the 2010 Currie Cup final. It really saddened me to see Pat having to retire due to concussion, aged 28 and in the prime of his career. Some will say that the sport we play is too dangerous, but I think it has become safer during my time at the top, with a lot of law changes aimed at making parents happy to see their sons joining rugby clubs.

I don't think that what happened to Pat was the fault of rugby; it was one of those things. You try your best to guard against serious injury, but sometimes you're just unlucky. I played alongside Pat in the game where he got the first serious concussion. It was the Test against Ireland at Newlands in 2016. Pat was on the front foot and chipped one down the middle; the next thing CJ Stander floored him and he was out cold.

I certainly don't think CJ meant to hurt him; he was trying to charge down the ball and got as high with his jump as he could. Pat's momentum made the collision look worse than it was, but seeing Pat lying there wasn't a pretty sight and we all just stopped. Pat had never been a drama queen, so when we saw him flat out we knew it was bad.

Back in 2012, all that was in the future. The Sharks got back to winning ways against the Highlanders and from then on we started getting rid of some bad habits and inculcating some good ones. Keegan was captain and because he and I had played together from a young age, we knew each other really well and treated each other as equals. But Keegan's a different guy and not everyone saw eye to eye with him. He was outspoken and if he felt strongly about something he would speak up.

But one day we sat down as a group and decided that enough was enough, everyone had to give their all for the team and it was time to turn the season around. We didn't just talk about it – we lived it every single day through training and took charge. Every weekend it got better and before we knew it we were on a roll.

We started climbing the log, and actually had a chance to end fourth and claim a home quarterfinal, but we lost to the Lions in Johannesburg. That meant we needed bonus-point wins in our last two home games, but as Ryan Kankowski used to say, 'The Sharks only start playing when we have a knife to our throats,' so we beat the Bulls 32–10 and the Cheetahs 34–15.

We ended up finishing sixth, which meant a trip to Brisbane to play the Reds, the defending Super Rugby champions. The Reds were a formidable team, but we played out of our skins and beat them in their own backyard. We scored three tries and Freddie Michalak kicked 15 points, including a drop goal. The final score was 30–17 and it was a happy team that boarded the plane back to South Africa.

The semi-final was against the Stormers in Cape Town. They had finished top of the log, so if they beat us they would have the opportunity to host a home final, which they had never done before. We, of course, were determined to make sure that didn't happen. We had played them twice in log play; they won 15–12 in Cape Town, while we beat them 25–20 in Durban, so it was always going to be a close contest.

On the day it was like a Test match. There was a moment when Eben Etzebeth collided with Bismarck and laid him out cold. I had never seen that happen to Bizzy before, but when the medical staff tried to coax him off the field he just refused.

He said, 'I'm not leaving this field.' He's the most stubborn guy I've ever met and he just put his foot down. This was in the days before concussion protocols and the 'ding-dong test' and he got up, told the medics he was fine, did a strength test and carried right on playing.

We continued where we had left off against the Reds and

I think the Stormers were a little complacent. To be fair, they had good reason to think we'd be tired because we had flown to Brisbane and back while they had had a week off to rest. I think they thought that, whatever happened, they'd finish us off in the last 20 minutes, but we just kept on playing ... all the way to the final.

During the week, we had spoken about the game and the effects of jet lag and Plum had said that they would assume we'd be tired and would try to run us off our feet. We actually didn't train that hard during the week – we wanted to make sure that we got our recovery right. We had three days off and even when we trained it was light work. The point was we wanted to be fresh for the challenge. We concentrated on winning territory and the set-pieces, and also had an ace up our sleeve in Louis Ludik, who was magnificent in the air at contestable kicks.

I remember looking at the Stormers guys after the final whistle and they were hurting, some of them sitting on the floor crying, because they had just dropped the biggest opportunity of their lives to host a Super Rugby final. They were broken and so was the whole of Cape Town. In retrospect, that was our final, because we couldn't celebrate – we had to jump on a plane to New Zealand to play the Chiefs in the final.

We took our bags, pre-packed for the final when we flew to Cape Town, so that we didn't have to go back to Durban, and boarded the plane for the final, which was in Hamilton. It was a gruesome trip, because we went straight from Newlands to the airport, flew from Cape Town to Joburg and then flew back across the time zones to Sydney. We stayed in Sydney until Thursday and then flew to Hamilton to get ready for the final. We were feeling good, but inevitably all the travel we had done in the last two weeks was bound to catch up with us at some point. It's not something that you can feel happening to you while you travel, but it creeps up on you.

For the first 20 minutes of the game the Chiefs just came at us and we couldn't keep up the pace, and I mean everyone, the whole team. They just bullied us the entire game and, in the end, it wasn't even a contest.

After about 50 minutes you could see how tired everyone was and we just wanted to get out of there. Our loss of 37–6 was a tough pill to swallow, but I think we learned a lot and it was an amazing accomplishment going backwards and forwards through the time zones.

In the long run, the impossible travel schedule imposed on the Sharks may have helped change the competition, although not necessarily for the better.

Most players and fans believe that the 12-team competition, which originated in 1996 and continued until 2005, was ideal. The Sharks contested the Super 14 final in 2007 and the Super 15 final in 2012, but the further expansion to 18 teams in 2016 has been widely criticised.

According to the competition's governing body, SANZAAR, the 18-team, four-'conference' format was an attempt to alleviate the kind of debilitating travel schedule experienced by the Sharks in 2012. In fact, it was a money-saving system, reducing the amount of costly international travel for teams and increasing the number of 'home derbies'.

The actual consequence of this expansion was that, in alternate years, South African teams avoided all the New Zealand or all the Australian teams until the knockout stages.

Chapter 14

MEET THE FAMILY

Today, Ku and I live in a designer home in Salt Rock, about 40 minutes up the highway from Kings Park. We have two children, a girl and a boy, Talumba (8) and Wangu (6).

Ku recalls how she found out that she was going to be a mother: '*I finished school and now I was studying law and the plan was to get married and then think about what we were going to do with the rest of our lives. But it turned out I was pregnant. I didn't think it was a big deal, but then I started falling asleep in lectures, so it was time to quit college.*

'*Talumba arrived a year into our marriage. Her name is from the language spoken by the Tonga who live in both Zimbabwe and Zambia and it means "thank you", or to be thankful. By this time we had moved to a new house in La Lucia, alongside a lot of other Sharks players. My mom spent a lot of time with us then, because as a new mother I literally knew nothing.*

'*Anyway, Talumba was growing and I was thinking about going back to college, so I went to the doctor to arrange some contraception*

and he did some tests and said, "I'm sorry, I can't give you contra-
ception, because you're pregnant." And that's how I discovered that
Wangu was going to join the family. Wangu means "my own" in the
Shona language and his full name is Wangutendai, which kind of
translates as, "My own little Tendai".'

My parents are frequent visitors, and on one of their trips to see
their grandchildren they shared their memories, especially of me
as a boy. My dad Felix Mtawarira is a sprightly 64 year old, who
plays tennis regularly against much younger opponents. He is a
well-educated man of above-average height, who speaks with a
similar booming voice to mine, albeit an octave higher.

My dad reflects: *'The Mtawariras are from Guruve, which is*
in the north of Zimbabwe, about 100 kilometres from Harare and
just before you get to the Zambezi Valley. We are Shona speakers,
but our second language is English. My grandfather came from
Chipinge, which is further south and on the border with Mozambique,
but he moved north to work for a man called Bill Francis on a farm
in Guruve, and that's where my father, Josiah Mtawarira, was born.

'My father was a tailor all his life. He sold clothes out of his
house to the people from the local villages – Chimbumu and Dinhidza,
which were very close to Guruve – mostly traditional African attire.
As he got better established, he was also contracted by some of the
local stores to supply them, so as children we always had clothes
that fitted us, but more importantly he made a good living and that
provided the money for us to go to school.

'My mother's name was Martha and she was from Dinhidza,
where my father used to sell clothes. They were married in the 1930s

and I was born in Guruve in 1956. I did my primary schooling there, but I moved to a neighbouring province to go to secondary school in Dzimwe. My best subject was Mathematics, so I think Tendai gets it from me, and I got my O Levels and A Levels, then did a full diploma at the Chartered Institute of Secretaries. I also did a master's in Business Administration, specialising in Financial Management. The second half of my studies were correspondence courses and that was just after Zimbabwe's independence in 1980.

'There was a lot of excitement in the rural areas about independence, because people felt that they would finally be given opportunities to better themselves, which they had not under the previous regime. There had been a lot of financial constraints and education, particularly in the rural areas, was vocational – carpentry, building, etc. – rather than academic. So if, like me, you wanted to be an accountant, or if you wanted to be a doctor, your prospects were limited.

'So when ZANU-PF came into power we thought we had a chance to empower ourselves more broadly. We had First-World ambitions, but over time our expectations were dashed, or perhaps not fully realised as Zimbabwe moved from democracy to dictatorship.

'My parents saw the need for my brothers and I to be properly educated and they kept us away from the bush wars and politics before independence. That was key, and when I started to earn a good wage I was able to help my family, particularly my siblings, to better themselves. My brothers came to live with me in Harare when I got my first job, which was as an agricultural officer. I had done a three-year agricultural course and my first job was working for

government, going out into the rural communities and teaching them modern methods in field and animal husbandry, market gardening and other things.

'My first pay packet was $72 and in the days before runaway inflation that was very good money. It was enough to sustain my brothers and I, and we were also able to send some groceries home. My brothers grew up and got their own professional jobs and to this day they are all doing fine.

'One day a work colleague of mine told me that she knew a chick who lived close to where I was living and she said she thought she would suit me. So in a way it was similar to what happened with Tendai and Ku. The difference was that I had been married before and had a child – Brian – but I was now divorced and my friend sensed a little frustration in me. She thought I needed someone of a specific character and that's how I got to meet Bertha. A love affair developed and I have not had any regrets.

'So we got married and now I had established a new family living in a suburb of Harare called Hatfield. It was quite a spacious four-bedroom house with an open-plan living area. Brian lived with us, and about a year after we married, Tendai was born. It didn't make a big difference, because we were a busy house anyway, with all my brothers living with us. I was now working for a large fertiliser company and when Tendai was born I had just been made a manager, so my earnings were enough to sustain the family and we never went hungry. That was important, because, as you know, Tendai was born hungry!

'There was a little bit of naughtiness in his character, but when he went to Prospect Primary he got some discipline. The teachers

141

at Prospect worked out quite quickly that the best way to deal with Tendai was to keep him occupied. That could lead to long days and I remember once my mother came to visit on the day that he had a rugby match and when he wasn't home by sunset she got very upset. She said, "Where is my grandchild?" and when I told her he was playing rugby she said, "This rubb-i-gee ..." – she couldn't say "rugby" – "This rubb-i-gee. What if he gets hurt?"

'I had never seen a game of rugby before he started playing, but we could see that rugby was good for him and it took a lot of steam out of him at the end of the day. He had developed as an aggressive character, but now that aggression had a purpose; that's the way I looked at it. And ultimately, of course, that helped him to get into Peterhouse. We also became aware that other people were seeing things in him that were worth nurturing and we spoke to him about it. We said, "People see something in you, but if you want to make rugby your career then you have to model your character around a person that is able to achieve great things in life. You've got to believe in the best and you have to be a character that wants to achieve, not one that chooses destruction by misbehaving." He took it to heart and he became the master of his own destiny.

'He began to change at Churchill and when he went to Peterhouse, in addition to being bright – remember, he got an A in his Maths A Level – he was at an institution that believed in character modelling. They really work on making people into complete human beings. I think you could sum it up by saying they focus you, aim you and make sure that you hit the target. As parents we did as much as we could, but Peterhouse has to take a whole lot of credit.

'Looking back, I think I am happy that I chose to send Tendai and

142

Brian to sporting schools, Churchill and Falcon. I had started play-
ing tennis and that influenced my decision. I still play, even though
I'm in my 64th year. Also in the back of my mind was the idea that
you can earn a good living from sport if you are good enough. Brian
blazed the trail for Tendai, playing rugby for Zimbabwe at Under-21
level, but he also was the leading triple-jumper in Zimbabwe while
still at school. They both had lots of natural talent, but it was helped
immensely by being in the right environment.

'Even so, when Tendai came home and told me that he had been
made an offer to go to the Sharks Academy I was a little taken
aback. I thought that in life when you aim for something that is too
high you may end up not achieving anything. My feeling was you
should aim a little lower and then work your way up. That was my
logic and I didn't know much about rugby, but I thought, "Why not
start a little lower, say with Griquas or the Pumas, and the progres-
sion might be better than going to a big union like the Sharks, where
you'll be a small fish in a big pool." Obviously, however, I was wrong!

'When he got on the bus to go to South Africa it didn't feel
right. His siblings were still studying: Ray was at Falcon, Lisa was
at primary school and Brian was at college and they all needed
financial support and now I had to try and find money to help Tendai
in South Africa. We were happy that he had a scholarship and that a
whole lot of things were going to be provided, but when he got there
he realised that there were many things he just couldn't afford. We
tried our level best to help him when he got in touch. Anything that
I had I would try and send his way, but not being physically present
made it a problem.

'He stayed in Durban for two years, partly because he couldn't

afford the travel costs to come home, but all that was forgotten when we flew down to watch him play for the first time. It wasn't the first time I had been in an aeroplane because I was in the Zimbabwe Air Force during national service, but I was ground crew and although I had been in and out of Dakotas and helicopters, I had never left the ground.

'Watching my own flesh and blood running onto the field at Kings Park was very emotional, especially because I knew that he had a lot more to show the world about what he was capable of. It seemed to me that he was the pivot in a group of players who showed that they really liked him. On the day that he phoned home to tell us that he had been picked to play for South Africa we were so excited, because we realised that he had reached the pinnacle. From that day we have scarcely missed watching a single game he's played. Normally he's playing on a Saturday, which means I can play my tennis at Alexander Sports Club and then watch the game with friends at the clubhouse.

'When he had to stop playing for the Springboks because of politics we were very upset. We couldn't understand how he could play 22 Tests and then be told he wasn't welcome, especially because Zimbabwe and South Africa are neighbours with an imaginary border. Basically, we are the same people and it was hard to swallow that a politician was responsible for doing this to a young man. We tried to give him support, but whenever we phoned him we could hear in his voice that something was amiss.

'But it came right eventually and then Tendai and Ku provided us with our first grandchild. We used to see each other a couple of times a year, but it's more frequent now that Tendai has business in Zimbabwe. We were invited to attend his 100th Test match in

Bloemfontein and that trip was definitely a moment for reflection. It said to me that if somebody charts their destiny and they really want to achieve their dreams, they can do it. Tendai was determined to get there, he worked hard for it, he continues to work hard and he has his reward.

'One day soon he's not going to be a professional rugby player anymore and we have always emphasised the need to prepare for life after rugby. It's a short professional career and the rest of your life is a long time. That's the stark reality.'

My mum, Bertha Mtawarira, is eight years younger than my dad and looks younger still. She laughs easily, speaks softly and likes to indulge her grandchildren whenever possible.

'I was born Bertha Kuhlengisa and the Kuhlengisa family are originally from KwaZulu-Natal, but my grandparents moved to Zimbabwe and that's where both my parents – Rhoda and James – were born. My father bought a farm in Murehwa, about an hour east of Harare, and I was born there in 1964. I was one of ten siblings, five boys and five girls, and we all had to help out on the farm. We grew maize, potatoes, beans and a few other crops, and we had some animals as well.

'It taught me how to work and so I have never had a problem. Right now I do all the housework at home; I don't have a maid or a gardener. I still wake up at 5am every day and I have a big yard at our house in Harare – 4 000 square metres – so I grow broad beans, maize and other vegetables. My parents are both late now, but my younger brother has taken over the farm in Murehwa. He still grows vegetables, but he has also started growing tobacco.

145

'When Tendai was born he was very big. The nurses at the hospital were calling to each other, "Come and see, come and see this big boy." He used to be very hungry and I didn't have enough milk for him, so by the time he was three months old I was already supplementing milk with porridge. He grew very quickly and he was always bigger than children the same age. At crèche and in Grade 1 he was a giant. It became a problem because he knew he was big and so he used to bully the other children. He was chased away from the crèche for fighting when he was not quite four years old. The teachers came to see me and we had to find a new crèche for him to go to.

'The fighting carried on when he went to primary school, but he wasn't chased away this time. Rugby was very important to his development; he had too much power and rugby provided an outlet for that power. When I watched him play, it was the first time I had seen rugby and I was very confused. Sometimes I would tell him not to play because it's too dangerous, but he refused and said, "Mum, that's my game."

'I played good sport when I was at school; I was in the netball team and I used to do athletics as well. My best events were the 100 and 400 metres, but I stopped sport after I left school. I was young when I married Felix, just 21. The lady who introduced us used to play with one of my sisters. I met him on the staff bus one day when I was with my sister going to work and I liked him from the start.

'After we got married and Tendai was born, next came Ray and then Lisa. It was a busy house with the children and Felix's brothers and sometimes there would be 10 of us sat at the supper table. I was a full-time mother and I did all the cooking, so mostly we would eat sadza, meat and vegetables. Tendai's favourite was my beef stew.

146

'When he went to South Africa I was very happy for him and when he told me he had a scholarship I was over the moon. I was brought up to believe that if you want something with all your heart, if you pray about it, nothing can stop you. I thank the Lord a lot and I'm very proud that my son believes the way I do and gives glory to God.

'When I first saw Ku at church I knew that she was the one for Tendai and, although it took a while before they spoke to each other, I was confident that this was God's will. When they got married I thought that my plans were now fulfilled! I like to spoil my grand-children, so I bring them surprises. Talumba likes dolls and Wangu likes cars.'

My younger brother, Ray, also pursued a professional rugby career, but it was sadly curtailed by serious injury. He followed me to Peterhouse and, in a further parallel, was persuaded to switch positions during his time at the Sharks Academy.

'The Sharks Academy gave me a bursary to come and try out. The training was tough and quite challenging. I was able to play for the Sharks at Under-19 and Under-21 level and when I gradu-ated in 2010 I was offered a professional contract by the Lions. I was a winger at school, but when I got to the Academy they moved me to flank, then at the Lions I became a hooker. At the final tri-als before the season started we were playing at the University of Johannesburg and I broke my neck in a scrum.

'I was bedridden for six weeks and couldn't play for a year, but the following year I decided to give the game another go. I played for Crusaders in Durban for about three months and then I tore

my anterior cruciate ligament in my knee. That's when I stopped for good; I think the game was trying to tell me something. The irony was that I'd never had a bad injury before, either at school or at the Academy. I went back to Zim for a while, but now I'm living in Johannesburg. I'm an entrepreneur and I specialise in digital marketing.'

Chapter 15

TOO MANY COACHES SPOIL THE SHARKS

After the heroics of the 2012 Super Rugby season, when the Sharks defied the odds to reach the final, the 2013 season was a huge disappointment. In retrospect, it was the start of a turbulent three years at Kings Park, a period that would see multiple coaches imposed on the players, together with financial insecurity at a union that had always prided itself on sound business principles.

The catalyst for change came from the boardroom, where it was decided that Brian van Zyl would step down as chief executive officer on the last day of February 2014. Van Zyl had been with the Sharks administration for 20 years and had risen to prominence during the glory years for the union in the 1990s. What shocked Sharks fans and the rugby community at large was Van Zyl's replacement, none other than 2007 World Cup-winning captain, John Smit.

Smit had retired from international rugby after the 2011 World Cup and played his final two seasons for Saracens in London. He was still appearing for Saracens when the Sharks announced on

April 16th, 2013, that he would succeed Van Zyl as CEO. Smit had been an outstanding leader of both the Sharks and Springboks, but had no boardroom experience at all. The idea was that he would join the Sharks on July 1st and that Van Zyl would mentor Smit for six months before stepping down.

In reality, things happened differently and Smit began his new role in the middle of a slump in fortunes for the Sharks, as they lost six Super Rugby games out of seven between April 13th and May 25th.

When we heard that John was coming on board as CEO it was a surprise to all the players. Obviously, he was a well-respected player who had achieved a lot in his career and, as such, we were quite excited and thought this could be a really good thing for the Sharks.

He was familiar with the setup, had grown up in the environment, knew most of the players, and it seemed there would be great synergy and we'd be able to work well together. In John's first week there was excitement in the whole Sharks organisation, but if there was one man who was nervous, it was Plum.

Two weeks after John arrived, Plum started feeling the heat. We were midway through the 2013 Super Rugby season and weren't playing well, having had some unexpected losses. One day we were training, with Plum coaching, and then the next day he was gone.

It was a difficult time because Plum was like a father figure to a lot of the players, especially me. It was really sad to see the way he was treated – because of what he had contributed to the

Sharks, he deserved a hell of a lot more. There was a lot of ugliness and it was not done in a professional manner.

There were no formal goodbyes and we were told at the next training session that Grant Bashford and Sean Everitt were taking over for the rest of the campaign and that Plum was gone.

As players, we found it very tough. We couldn't understand why it was handled the way it was. John came to talk to us and tried to clear the air, but it still didn't make much sense. There comes a point, however, when you have to get on with the job; you're paid to play rugby and we had to find a way to perform on the field, despite what was happening. So you close that stuff away in a little cabinet somewhere at the back of your mind and just carry on.

Things didn't really get any better at the Sharks. After Plum, there were others who were not dealt with very professionally.

One guy who was very influential, for instance, was Mark Steele, our conditioning coach. He had been in the setup for 10 years and I had known him since I started at the Academy, as had a number of other players. Mark made a huge contribution to the Sharks and he was also treated badly.

Again, we never had a chance to say goodbye. One day he was there, the next he had gone and we couldn't understand it. This was a guy who deserved a medal and he was treated horribly.

So it was a terrible time for the players, but they still delivered, because although we didn't do very well in Super Rugby that year, we won the Currie Cup. Brendan Venter came in at John's behest and tried to make things better. He sat us down and was forthright with us – Brendan doesn't beat around the bush. He said he knew things had been stuffed up, but needed to know what we, as players, were feeling about it.

And we told him and he said, 'Okay, we can deal with that.' He said, 'I will be your voice to John and to the guys at the top. You guys can come and tell me what you feel, but in the end you must know that I'm going to demand the same from you. I'm going to demand excellence on the field.'

We agreed that Brendan would handle all the off-the-field stuff – and he was as good as his word. At the time, Odwa Ndungane had heard that they wanted to get rid of him when his contract came up at the end of the year, but Brendan said, 'Don't worry, I've got you.' And, sure enough, he arranged for Odwa's contract to be extended.

So, things were happening, but in the end Brendan wasn't around long enough. He was commuting from his medical practice in Stellenbosch – his family was based down there – and for him to move to Durban was just never going to happen because there wasn't a big enough incentive.

So it was that the Sharks were in the market for a new head coach, or in the modern parlance, Director of Rugby. Smit had won a World Cup with Jake White at the helm and so there were few surprises when White's name was thrown into the ring.

White, somewhat controversially, had been fired by Saru after victory at the 2007 World Cup. Subsequently, he set up a coaching business and did work with various clubs and unions, but in 2012 he signed a four-year contract with the Brumbies in Australia.

In 2013 the Brumbies went all the way to the final before narrowly losing 27–22 to the Chiefs in Hamilton. White's methods clearly worked and it should be remembered that he took over the Springboks in 2004, at a low point in South Africa's rugby history, and ended his four-year tenure with World Cup glory. Midway through his second year in Canberra, White chose not to honour his contract with the Brumbies and instead came to Durban. For outsiders, it may have seemed like a marriage made in heaven, but it was a different story for the Sharks players.

So that was when Jake White arrived at the Sharks, towards the end of the 2013 Currie Cup season. I didn't get to play much Currie Cup, because most of the time I was away with the Boks, but I picked up that the players weren't happy with Jake's methods – and discovered that first hand when the 2014 Super Rugby season began.

There was a lot of commotion in the camp and a lot of unhappiness, because Jake treated us like schoolboys. He wanted us at Kings Park at 7am and insisted that we be there until 6pm.

Jake was set in his ways and wasn't prepared to listen to anyone. He banned alcohol completely. Now, I'm not a big drinker, but there are a lot of guys who enjoy a beer after a game and they were not happy.

Then Jake introduced all these theories from the Brumbies, the team he coached before he came to the Sharks. Everything he said to us was about the Brumbies, and even our plays on the field were from the Brumbies. The funniest thing was that when we played the Brumbies that season they would call the same play as us!

We were dumbfounded. It seemed like everything Jake said to us would include the line, 'At the Brumbies we used to ...' He would show us clips of them training, reviews of their games, whatever, and the boys would be fed up. 'We don't want to watch the Brumbies,' they would say, 'we're better than them.' John, of course, had won a World Cup with Jake and he believed in his methods, so he would try to patch things up with the players when they came to him to complain.

John would speak directly to Jake, but things never changed and Jake carried on treating everyone as though they didn't know what they were doing, and that included the management team. John tried to manage the situation and cautioned Jake a few times, because when you get the management team and the players constantly coming to you to complain about the coach, then you know there's something wrong.

I've always been the kind of person who can pull myself away from the craziness that's happening around me and focus on the job at hand. At the end of the day, I know that my performance is what's important. I know that if I play well the team will benefit. And we actually had a decent 2014 Super Rugby season and made it to the playoffs, even with all the nonsense going on with Jake.

We played the Highlanders in Durban. We won that, but couldn't beat the Crusaders in Christchurch in the semi-final. So John had to look elsewhere for a coach and in the end he brought in Gary Gold.

Gold had been part of Peter de Villiers's coaching team during his four-year stint as Springbok coach. Gold was highly regarded as an analyst and coached at Bath and in Japan for the Kobelco Steelers before signing for the Sharks.

It was agreed that Gold should see out his contract with the

Steelers, but that meant that he only arrived in Durban three weeks ahead of the 2015 Super Rugby season.

Gary was a little flustered when he arrived because he had to try to get everything together quickly and there was no time. I had known him a long time and we had worked together at the Boks. He was the kind of guy whose company I enjoyed, but I also had a lot of respect for him.

He was thrown into the deep end, with a lot of stuff going on behind the scenes, and he just couldn't get the team firing together. Matters weren't helped by injuries to some key players such as Pat Lambie and Pieter-Steph du Toit, and then Marcell Coetzee announced that he was moving to Ulster and the Sharks weren't too happy about that. Ruan Botha had just joined the Sharks and he broke his hip in a warm-up game.

With all of this, we found it hard to get going and do things the way we were used to within the Sharks setup. There was a lot of confusion in the camp, with some not really understanding which way we were going, because there was no proper direction. As players, we were wondering what the heck was going on and why all these bad decisions were being made.

Since the firing of Plum, we had had three coaches in three years with no input from the players. We were all just playing a guessing game.

Gold's first season in charge never got going. The team lost three of their first four matches, all to South African franchises, and then ran into disciplinary problems.

Against the Chiefs in Durban, both Bismarck du Plessis and Frans Steyn received red cards. Two weeks later Jean Deysel also received his marching orders at Kings Park as the Sharks were humiliated 52–10 by the Crusaders.

All three Springboks received lengthy bans, which did not make the season any easier for Gold's men. They finished eleventh on the log, a humiliating position for a team packed with talent and international experience.

Things didn't improve for Gold in the Currie Cup, either. Having won the tournament in 2008, 2010 and 2013, in 2015 they failed to reach the knockout stages for the first time in a decade. Gold remained at the helm for the 2016 Super Rugby tournament, the first to be played under the new Conference System. The Sharks scraped into the playoffs in last place, finishing eighth on the log, before being humiliated 41–0 by the Hurricanes in the Wellington quarterfinal.

Gold then assumed the title of Director of Rugby and Robert du Preez took over as Currie Cup coach for the 2016 competition. Du Preez had been coaching Pukke – North West University – in the Varsity Cup before coming to the Sharks, but his twin sons, Daniel and Jean-Luc, were already at the union, having been schooled at Kearsney College and come through the Sharks' age-group structures. Once again in 2017 the Sharks missed out on the playoffs, after losing to the Lions in the final round of log play. It was the final straw and Gold left the Sharks with a year to go on his contract.

After three tumultuous years at the helm, John Smit had already stepped down as CEO. He announced his decision at the end of May, stating that he would step aside at the end of the year *because he wanted to spend more time with his family.*

Brian van Zyl, Smit's predecessor, wrote an open letter to The Mercury, *Durban's daily newspaper, suggesting that the real reason was that the Sharks were in a perilous financial position. A figure of R40 million was mentioned by Van Zyl as the true debt level at the union due to some poor financial decisions.*

Smit responded by saying that the Sharks had experienced financial difficulties before he came on board in 2013 and that the need to pay market-related salaries to keep players from leaving to play in Europe and Japan had subsequently made things more difficult.

Whatever the true facts of the case, there can be little doubt that Smit's three years in charge coincided with unhappy times in the dressing room. With Gold and Smit out of the picture, Du Preez became the Sharks Super Rugby coach in 2017, and at the time of writing he is into his third season in charge.

Robert being here for a third season in itself has helped to settle things down, but what gives me great hope is that our junior teams have become very competitive. Through the last decade, they were never very consistent, but in 2018 both the Under-19s and Under-21s had excellent seasons. Kids such as Phepsi Buthelezi, Sanele Nohamba and JJ van der Mescht have come through in a way that shows that the province still has great talent at grass-roots level in the schools.

Dick Muir came back for a season as an assistant coach under Robert and, for me, that was special, because Dick stands out as the guy I would go to war for. I enjoyed Dick for his sound management of the players and the way he created a great environment for the team. It was awesome to have him back and we cracked a few jokes – it's just a shame his stay was so short-lived.

LEFT: Regan Hoskins, president of the South African Rugby Union. He stood up for me under political pressure. (© Steve Haag)

BELOW: It's not always serious on Bok tours. Left to right: Pierre Spies, Jannie du Plessis, me and Bakkies Botha. (© Steve Haag)

ABOVE: A moment with the Currie Cup, 2013. (© Steve Haag)

BELOW: The Sharks celebrate their Currie Cup win against Western Province, Newlands, 2013. (© Steve Haag)

ABOVE: Celebrating Lood de Jager's try against Japan, before things began to fall apart, 2015 World Cup, Brighton. (© Steve Haag)

LEFT: Happy to have a bronze medal at the 2015 Rugby World Cup. (© Mike Hewitt/Getty Images)

Bryan Habana with the selfie stick as we celebrate beating Argentina to finish third in the 2015 World Cup. (© Steve Haag)

LEFT: One of my father figures, John Plumtree. (© Steve Haag)

ABOVE: One of the good guys, Gary Gold, during his time as Director of Rugby at the Sharks. (© Steve Haag)

You'll believe a man can fly; lifting Etienne Oosthuizen against the Hurricanes at Kings Park. (© Steve Haag)

ABOVE: I get a lot of this; posing for selfies after a Sharks game. (© Steve Haag)

RIGHT: Talumba (left) and Wangu, at my 100th Test, Bloemfontein, 2018.
(© Steve Haag)

LEFT: The Mtawarira family at my 100th Test: Ku, Wangu, me and Talumba.
(© Steve Haag)

BELOW: Friends and family in the stands at my 100th Test, Bloemfontein, 2018.
(© Steve Haag)

Playing in the Black Panther outfit, Kings Park, 2019. (© Steve Haag)

Chapter 16

THE 2015 WORLD CUP

Saru parted ways with Peter de Villiers at the end of the 2011 World Cup and, as early as the second week of January in 2012, Heyneke Meyer had been touted in the press as the next Springbok coach. Unable to keep the appointment secret any longer, Meyer was formally announced in the position on January 27th, and given a four-year contract by Saru.

It was Meyer who had masterminded the resurgence of the Blue Bulls Rugby Union in the early years of the new millennium, first as coach and then as Director of Rugby. Under Meyer, the Bulls became the most-feared provincial union in the world, winning the Super Rugby title three times in four years, the first of those at the expense of the Sharks in 2007. A plethora of great players emerged at that time, including Victor Matfield, Fourie du Preez, Danie Rossouw and Bakkies Botha.

Unfortunately for Meyer, all four announced their international retirement at the end of the 2011 World Cup, together with John Smit and Jaque Fourie. This left a huge gulf in terms of experience and

Meyer subsequently decided that he could not do without Matfield and Du Preez. He persuaded both out of retirement midway through his term of office and they became key members of the squad that would go to the 2015 World Cup. After much behind-the-scenes wrangling, the Meyer era began in June 2012 with a three-Test series against England and a new captain, Stormers centre Jean de Villiers.

At the Bulls, Heyneke Meyer was known as a great manager of people who knew how to get a team working together. When a new Springbok coach takes over there is definitely a big fear amongst the players. What if he doesn't like you? But I think that, in the end, performance is everything and my philosophy is that as long as I'm on top of my game then my performance speaks for itself.

Heyneke was very good to me and we had an excellent relationship. There would be weekly one-on-ones and that meant that you knew where you stood and what he expected of you. He praised me for being a good team man and for never complaining. His dream was to get to the World Cup and win it, and while he didn't realise that dream I can honestly say the four years leading up to the 2015 World Cup were the happiest of my Springbok career.

One of Heyneke's great accomplishments was to bring Fourie du Preez and Victor Matfield out of retirement to play for the Boks again. That didn't cause any resentment in the team because they were legends of the game and we regarded them as coaches as much as players. As captain, Jean de Villiers was easy-going and approachable and knew how to relate to people. He was particularly good with youngsters coming into the setup for the first time.

He was always ready to give his time and answer questions and, most importantly, he was a fun guy.

Jean's biggest problem was injuries, which always seemed to come at the wrong time. In 2014 he injured his knee before the June internationals and was always in a race against time to be ready for the World Cup.

Jean de Villiers was very generous about playing alongside Beast. He says, 'He is the Beast on the field, but off the field he's just the most gentle guy you'll ever meet and a fantastic person, a great ambassador for the country and an awesome player. Jannie and Bismarck played a lot of rugby with Beast and they always spoke about "The Shake" before the game. When you stand there singing the national anthem and you can feel Beast is shaking, you know he's ready.'

Ah, yes, The Shake. You can't see it from the stands, but it's like my body is vibrating. I can't help it.

John Smit had another way of checking on Beast's readiness for battle. He says, 'As captain, I used to hope that early in the game someone from the opposition would kick him or scratch him or do something to upset him, because once he was worked up there wasn't a rugby player I've ever played against who would be able to contain the Beast; when he got mad, he was unstoppable.'

I guess that's true. My eyes go red, I see blood and it's war. And that, I think, is the kind of motivation you need to get you through a game, especially when it's the World Cup at stake.

Ahead of the World Cup we'd had a big send-off in Johannesburg. Lots of people turned up at Montecasino to see us and there was a lot of hype about the team and what

161

it was going to achieve. On the other side of the coin, however, there was also some controversy, with politicians claiming that the team did not represent South Africa, because it didn't have enough players of colour. That kind of tainted the whole moment and I remember Heyneke feeling like the whole world was about to collapse on him.

As a team, we tried to dwell on the positives and once in Eastbourne we had a good week on the training field. Nobody gave much thought to the politics crap, and perhaps underestimated the challenge it posed. Maybe we were guilty of focusing on what the media was saying rather than on what we were facing on Saturday, so we began the World Cup with the lowest of all lows: losing to Japan in Brighton.

One team's low is another's high and Japan's extraordinary 34–32 defeat of South Africa remains their finest moment in international rugby. It also gave the World Cup the kind of dream start that organisers love, convincing the sceptics that miracles can happen in rugby. Japan – the Brave Blossoms, as they are known at home – were coached by Eddie Jones, who had been to the final with the Wallabies in 2003 and as assistant to Jake White in the Springboks' victorious campaign in 2007. After beating the Boks, Japan went on to record pool wins against both Samoa and the USA, but were unable to qualify for the quarterfinals.

I remember running onto the field and I was feeling good, excited, proudly singing the national anthem, and I actually had a really good game – but no one's ever going to remember that! Things started well, but Japan scored a try from a maul on the half-hour and our whole forward pack looked at each other as if

162

to say, what the heck just happened? This isn't supposed to happen to a Springbok pack. There was silence and nobody really stood up. I think we always thought we'd find a way to win.

We were up at half-time, and then Lood de Jager scored a really good try early in the second half, but Japan kept in the game with penalties and kept chipping away at the lead. It was 19–all in the 54th minute when Heyneke made the decision to replace the whole front row: Jannie, Bizzy and me. Trevor Nyakane replaced me and Coenie Oosthuizen took over from Jannie. The game changed when their fullback scored Japan's second try with about 10 minutes left. We were thinking that the tries were going to come, but we never got far enough ahead and before we knew it time was getting less and less and Japan were the ones putting the pressure on us. We started making more errors and our opponents fed off the crowd, which would erupt every time Japan did something good.

Then Coenie got a yellow card for repeated infringements by the team. That was in the 79th minute and I had to come back on to replace him, because there was a scrum five metres from our line. The crowd was going nuts, but at that point we were leading 32–29 and I was absolutely convinced we'd win. We went hard at them in the scrum, almost turned it over, but they just managed to get the ball out and played all the way to one edge of the field. We went to sleep a bit, I think, and they played the ball all the way back the other way, only for the wing, Karne Hesketh, to run around JP and score the winning try.

We couldn't believe what had happened, none of us. I looked around the field and it was as if everyone had had a near-death experience. This was not what we were about and definitely not the way we wanted to start the campaign. We were shocked. Afterwards, when we got to the dressing room, Heyneke was distraught; he didn't know what to say. Some guys were actually crying and no one said anything until we asked the coaching team to step out of the room. Then Victor stood up and said, 'Hey, guys, we can decide right now that this is the end of our World Cup, fly home and let another team take our place. If that's what you want, walk out of the room now.'

Nobody moved; then we went round the room, one by one, and everyone had to say something. When it was my turn I committed myself to the team and vowed to do my very best, give more of myself and dig deeper for this team to make sure that we go all the way. We made a decision in that changing room that we were going to turn this into the biggest comeback ever and win the World Cup. From that moment on the team's whole mindset changed.

It wasn't really a case of chasing Heyneke out or removing him from the picture, but rather the moment that the players took charge. Victor and Fourie, in particular, assumed a lot of responsibility, which was of course ironic because it was Heyneke who had persuaded them out of retirement in the first place.

In fact, Matfield and Du Preez were to assume ever more responsibility, because Jean de Villiers' wretched luck at World Cups continued, the captain breaking his jaw in the next match against Samoa, when he collided with Tim Nanai-Williams. Du Preez assumed the captaincy from that point on and, in the scrumhalf's absence, Matfield took the captain's armband for the bronze medal match against Argentina. It was noticeable in the fallout from the

Japan defeat that the Springboks began to play a more expansive game, one that the press and many supporters had been asking to see for a long time.

We have been criticised at times over the years for being one-dimensional and that at times we were too predictable. That probably contributed to us being beaten by Japan. Eddie Jones spoke to us after the game and said that they had been training for this game from the moment the pool draws had been made more than two years previously. He said, 'We knew exactly what you guys were going to do because you've been playing the same way for the past four years. We knew Schalk was going to come around the corner and we just practised smashing you guys back so that you couldn't get any momentum.'

And it was fair criticism – we had become too predictable and had to change our game after the Japan Test. We needed to move away from the tactic of just smashing the guy in front of you and find a way to move the ball away from contact, specifically so that we could remove the pressure from a guy like Schalk, who had the skills to be a good playmaker and didn't have to try to bash into seven forwards. So it was a question of letting him attract those forwards, then playing it to the back where there was now more space. We didn't feel the need to make really big changes, because our set-pieces had always been great – it was just a question of being more creative in our use of the ball.

As it turns out, Eddie Jones was a Beast fan. He says, 'I think he's one of those iconic players in South African rugby. He fought his way through and modernised the prop's game. He was really one of the first props that was a great ball carrier and he's been able to combine that with solid scrummaging, and that's what has made him an indispensable member of the Springbok side for a long time.'

So, after that defeat by Japan, we left Brighton and headed to Birmingham for our next game against Samoa. We had decided that we were not going to talk about the Japan Test, not even watch the video. No one would tweet, we would get off social media, and not read the papers – just complete tunnel vision, focusing on Samoa.

We trained hard on the Monday – really physical – then trained hard again Tuesday, had Wednesday off and trained like machines again on Thursday and Friday. By Saturday we were ready to kill Samoa. And our forwards hurt them properly; some folks had to get off the field. The first 20 minutes was all about expressing our anger at what had happened against Japan, so we got stuck into them and by the end of the game everything was pretty much back on track.

From there we moved on north to Newcastle to play Scotland and did enough there to win comfortably. The forwards provided a good platform, and we hurt them at set-piece time, which allowed the backs to score some good tries. But by now we had our eyes on the final and, to be honest, beating Scotland seemed rather insignificant. We went on to beat the USA 64–0, but that also seemed to be just part of the process. Now we were in the quarterfinals, but it wasn't like we were basking in the sun, thinking we had achieved our goal – our mindset was to win the next one and then the next one and ultimately to win the World Cup.

We had come a long way in a short time. After we lost to

Japan, people thought we wouldn't make the knockout stages, saying things like this was the worst Bok team ever. They were trying to split us as a group and the UK media also climbed on the bandwagon. All of that, though, just made us stronger. We played Wales in the quarters at Twickenham and it was tightly contested. Wales kicked well and Dan Biggar scored their first try with a really good piece of play. He kicked a little up-and-under, just a chip that caught us napping, collected it and scored.

We then traded penalties and there was a huge physical confrontation up front. We made a lot of errors and we knew that it was going to go right down to the wire. We won it right at the end with a good scrum. Duane Vermeulen broke off and drew their right wing, then did a little back flip to Fourie du Preez who scored in the corner. It showed again that there is no substitute for composure and experience when you are under pressure.

At 19–18 down with five minutes left, Du Preez's try snatched victory from the jaws of defeat. The Boks won 23–19 and their reward was a semi-final against the All Blacks at Twickenham. The defeat by Japan seemed light years away. The Boks had now won four in a row and the team that had committed themselves in the Brighton changing room to the greatest comeback ever was on a roll.

And for 50 minutes the impossible dream of beating New Zealand to reach the final was in sight. Four Handré Pollard penalties sent the underdogs into the dressing room with a 12–7 half-time lead. The defending champions were rattled by the dynamic Bok defence and something akin to the 1995 final between the same two sides seemed to be on the cards.

Early in the second half, the great Dan Carter at flyhalf slotted a drop goal and the All Blacks hit the front for the first time with a Beauden Barrett try in the 52nd minute. After that, the Boks struggled to get out of their own half and the game slowly slipped away.

We play the All Blacks on a regular basis, but in a World Cup the stakes are always higher. It was the road to the final and, as such, it was a moment that many of the players wouldn't get back. It was pretty much everything for this team and in the end we were really charged up. We were ready to throw everything at them and everyone was switched on right from the onset. That was our final.

In the first half we were pretty comfortable, defending really well, frustrating them so that they weren't getting any go-forward ball. We were hurting them by playing proper Springbok rugby and you could see they were feeling it. There's no secret to how you play against the All Blacks; you have to impose yourself. They don't like getting smashed in the contact and you have to make sure that you hurt them, because what they want is freedom to play and you can't play if you're always on the back foot. So that's always our mentality when we play them; starve them of the ball and when they do happen to get it, smash them. The set-piece is huge and we have to make sure we win that facet of play.

And for three quarters of that game we were there, putting them in that uncomfortable space, and that's what made the defeat hurt so much. They won by pinning us in our own 22 for the last 15 minutes. We couldn't exit and it started to drizzle and, because of the pressure they were putting on us, we just couldn't kick the ball far enough.

Pollard had reduced the deficit to two points in the 58th minute, but Carter restored a five-point gap on the hour. Remarkably,

Pat Lambie's 69th-minute penalty was the only score by either side in the last quarter. Ultimately, the team that had lost by two points against Japan a month previously lost by two again (18–20) after putting up one of the bravest backs-to-the-wall efforts ever seen at a World Cup. There is no doubt the best side won, and there is also no doubt that the Boks gave the All Blacks a far harder game than Australia managed in the final, which ended 34–17 in New Zealand's favour.

Our defeat was devastating and it took a few weeks for me to recover. Problem was we had to play Argentina in the 3rd/4th playoff match six days later. Heyneke gave us four days off and we trained for the first time again on the Thursday.

In the break we split up and I was able to spend time with my family, which was probably the best medicine for me. Ku and the kids were there and I have lots of extended family in London. My mum's sister's kids all moved there when the situation in Zim became really bad about 20 years ago. There were no opportunities and no jobs in Zimbabwe and my extended family were pretty smart because, like me, they had done the Cambridge syllabus, so they had qualifications that were accepted in Britain.

They weren't the only ones, of course; lots of Zimbabweans emigrated to Britain at the same time and settled, married, and had kids, so I have plenty of cousins over there. It made it difficult at the World Cup because I had to organise crazy numbers of tickets for them all. I would say I have at least 50 relatives there, so I just couldn't please everyone, but I did what I could.

Chapter 17

BEING THE BEAST

The persona of the Beast is something I lock away somewhere and then I bring it out in a match situation. When I'm at home, I'm a dad to my children and a good husband to my wife, so I have to separate the two, because I can't be aggressive all the time. But when I'm at work and I pull on the Sharks or Springbok jersey, that's my Superman time and I flick the switch to become the Beast. 'He' is not someone else; he's my alter ego, a different version of myself.

I always had lots of power in me as a kid and when the Beast came along it was a way of channelling my aggression. Of course, 90% of the people I meet don't even know that my real name is Tendai; they only know the Beast. I'm not the only player who switches personalities that way; there are a few I've played with and against. For instance, Craig Burden is a good friend of mine and a really nice guy off the field, but as soon as he gets onto the field he also has a switch that is flicked.

I won't have a problem controlling the Beast after I stop

playing. I'll always have ways and means of channelling my passion, my energies and my values. It's been good to me from a marketing perspective; it's unique and fits perfectly with the kind of person I am.

One of the tricks the Beast has up his sleeve is lifting a lock and holding him in the air while we wait for the ball to come down. The first few times I did it the television commentators thought I was saving the lock from falling over backwards, but it's not as haphazard as it might look on screen.

The first person I lifted in a game was actually Steven Sykes, but everyone remembers Anton Bresler, because there's a famous picture of me lifting him in the game against the Crusaders in London. There's another of me lifting Keegan Daniel in a Currie Cup game. I had done it a lot at training before I tried it in a game and it was just a question of practice. My natural ability and strength, allied to working in the gym, made it possible.

The guy in the air can get very scared, but I try to tell him not to worry: 'Don't stress, I've got you.' I've never dropped anyone yet and it's a kind of pact I have with my locks. I tell them before the game that if they want to go for a high ball and they feel it's too far away, then don't stress, just go for it. It's not a move that we call; it just depends on the kicker and, obviously it's mainly from kick-offs that it happens.

I've seen Trevor Nyakane do the same move, but I don't think it's as perfect as mine! I guess it's my trademark. If you're strong enough you can give it a go, but it's dangerous, so be careful. We have a session devoted to kick-receiving most weeks, so I practise it regularly.

We played the Lions in Joburg a couple of years ago and I lifted Stephan Lewies twice, so they started complaining to the ref about it. The Lions players felt I was milking it by holding him up too long, which with the laws against tackling a player in the air meant that they couldn't touch him. It's general play so it's within the law for me to hold him there, but the ref asked if I wouldn't mind putting him down a second or so earlier.

In 2018 I played my 100th Test match almost exactly 10 years after I played my first. That averages out at 10 Tests a year and if you consider I missed a whole year with the wrangling over my eligibility, then it's a record I'm very proud of. My 99th match was against England in Johannesburg and we had to come back from a big deficit to win. It was a three-Test series so as it turned out my 100th game was crucial, meaning we would either win the series with a game to spare, or go to the third Test at 1–1.

In the circumstances, it was a big week for me, not just a case of running out into the stadium on Saturday afternoon and acknowledging the crowd. Springbok coach Rassie Erasmus came to me early on and said they would be keeping the media off my back, because it was also a big week for the team. He also said, with a twinkle in his eye, that they'd chosen to play my 100th Test in Bloemfontein because he didn't want too many distractions!

It was the perfect setting and there weren't too many people trying to talk to me, just a few phone calls; our media officer, Rayaan Adriaanse, kept things quiet. This meant I was able to focus on the job at hand during training and put the 100th Test scenario on the back-burner. But there were about 30 members of my family in Bloem all week and they were so excited. I had to get them all nice gear, Springbok jerseys and beanies, and make sure they had hotel rooms. Fortunately Asics came on board and they put together personalised jerseys for everyone ahead of time.

By Thursday, however, the goose-bumps were there. I had to do a press conference with Rassie, speak a little about what it means to play 100 Tests, and I got quite emotional thinking about what a long road I had travelled to get there, the challenges I had faced, and the people who had inspired me and walked the road with me.

On Friday André Venter came to hand out the Springbok jerseys. André is in a wheelchair now after a terrible illness, but he was a hard man in his time, a Springbok legend, and to this day he is filled with energy and passion. He spoke about what it means to be a Springbok and then he talked about my 100th cap. He said mine was an inspiring story, one that gave hope to the whole country and to people in every sphere of life, and that it proved what you could achieve with hard work and dedication. When he gave me my jersey and it had *100 caps* on the chest, I was completely overcome.

The next day all my family and friends were in the stands when I walked out onto the field with my children, both of them wearing the *Beast, Number 1* jersey. It was funny because Wangu was super keen to get out there, but Talumba didn't want to go at all. Wangu was saying, 'Let's go, papa, when are we going to start playing?' He thought he was coming out to play, but Talumba wanted to turn around and that's why I had to pick them up. Sometimes it helps to be strong; I said, 'There's no turning back now,' and obviously they were confused by all the attention they were getting and the noise, but it actually helped me to relax because it helped defuse all the tension.

The kids ran off after the pictures had been done and before I knew it, the national anthem was playing and I had to tune in to Test-match mode. The adrenalin was pumping and my heart was racing, but fortunately it wasn't a medical problem this time, so I grabbed the guys and pulled them around me and then it was time to go.

England scored early, just as they had done in Joburg the week before, and soon we were 12–0 down. But an opportunity came my way soon after that and I had a nice run through a sleeping defender. I was stopped about six metres from the line, but got the ball away to RG Snyman; he then passed it to Duane Vermeulen and Duane scored. From there we just kept on chipping away at them and in the end we won the game comfortably.

England came back to win the third Test, but we had already clinched the series, so in some respects it was a little like the series against the British and Irish Lions in 2009. As a professional rugby player, you can never afford to lose motivation, but once you've achieved what you set out to do, sometimes you just can't help it.

Looking back over 100 Tests, there are some I struggle to remember, but others stand out and I can still relive every detail. These are the special ones for me.

South Africa 53, Australia 8, Johannesburg, August 30th, 2008

We scored eight tries and put them to the sword. Jongi Nokwe scored four of the tries on the left wing. Sadly, he only played one more Test and that was the one we lost against the Lions a year later. But this Ellis Park win was a real highlight for me because it was in my debut season and showed how much potential we had in the squad.

England 6, South Africa 42, Twickenham, November 22nd, 2008

We were 20 points up at half-time and it was one of those games where everything went our way: the ball bounced in our favour, passes stuck, and for the rest of the game it seemed like England just wanted to get back into the changing room as soon as possible to end the humiliation.

South Africa 26, British and Irish Lions 21, Durban, June 20th, 2009

In the first Test of the series the Lions players made the mistake of slagging off the Springbok forwards. We taught them a lesson and John Smit, playing at tighthead, scored a try!

South Africa 28, British and Irish Lions 25, Pretoria, June 27th, 2009

It was 25–25 with time up on the clock when Morné Steyn kicked a penalty from inside our own half to win the game. He had come off the bench in what was only his second Test match, but it never looked like he was going to miss. We had lost the series the last time the Lions came to South Africa in 1997, so this was sweet revenge.

New Zealand 29, South Africa 32, Hamilton, September 12th, 2009

This was the game when we won the Tri Nations for the third time and also beat the All Blacks for the third time in the season. We haven't won the championship since, so this remains a truly memorable occasion. Frans Steyn knocked over some crazy long-range penalties, Jean de Villiers got one of his famous intercept tries and we partied big time at the final whistle.

South Africa 56, Samoa 23, Pretoria, June 22nd, 2013

Samoa might not be one of the super powers of world rugby, but they're a tough team to play against because they're fast and skilful and you have to beat them physically or they'll run all over you. That day we imposed ourselves on them, played the perfect game and the scoreline tells the tale.

South Africa 27, New Zealand 25, Johannesburg, October 4th, 2014

We were all over New Zealand in the first half and built up a big lead, but then they started coming back and before we knew it we were behind, with time running out. We received a penalty in our own half and somebody volunteered to take it, but Pat Lambie stepped in and said, 'This is my kick.' When it went over, Pat went crazy, which was out of character really, but that's the difference between beating Samoa and beating the All Blacks. Also, it had been a long time since we'd beaten them, so it really sticks in the mind.

Hopefully, my best Test memories of all are still ahead of me. The year 2019 is a World Cup one and I am still a contracted Springbok, but you never get complacent, because there's never any guarantee. Rassie said last year, 'Don't ever get comfortable.' You need to meet the standards and this year is going to be huge. There's lots of competition for my place and so I'm focusing on being good, week in and week out. There are certain aspects of my game that I have to develop, so I'm constantly looking for feed-back, working with the coaches and analysing my game. I keep on being hard on myself and eventually that's what it comes down to: hard work.

Contributing to the team is what it's about, so while starting a game is great, you can also contribute off the bench. I'm at a different stage of my career to some of the other guys and what I really want to do is be part of a winning team. I won't lie, being the best is everything to me, but sometimes you have to put your ego to one side to help the team. What I do in Super Rugby is going to set me up for what comes after that. What you hope is that when the time comes, it will take care of itself.

This is my thirteenth Super Rugby season and the Sharks have honoured me by putting my Super Rugby number, 144, on the away jersey. I'm the 144th Sharks player to have played in Super Rugby and on April 5th 2019, I passed Adriaan Strauss's 156 caps to become the most capped South African player ever in the competition. Adriaan is a good friend and was always a great man to be on tour with. He's a really good guitarist and an even better singer, and if he'd never played rugby he could have made it as a professional musician.

The 157th cap game was a real stand-out one for me. We played the Lions in Johannesburg, where we hadn't won for five years. It was a Friday night and the weather was dreadful, but we put on a vintage Sharks performance, winning 42–5.

The Sharks' chief operating officer, Eduard Coetzee, played five seasons at loosehead for the franchise and was one of those who helped in Beast's conversion to prop. He says that one day he was asked by Dick Muir to have a look at two new prop forwards who were playing in the Under-21 side. 'Dick wanted my opinion on whether they would make it or not, so I walked over to where they were training and watched. It was Beast and Pat Cilliers and it didn't take me long to make up my mind. I told Dick, "These boys can play," and since they both became Springboks, I guess I was right.'

Coetzee also spoke about why the Sharks had chosen to honour Beast by putting his number on the away jerseys. He says, 'Beast's contribution to the Sharks cannot only be limited to the field of play, but also the role he's played off it. He has been a role model and mentor for numerous young props, as well as players who have come through the system and who were able to learn so much from him, both as a player and human being.'

There is pressure attached to being honoured like that, but also pride, and it is a huge privilege to be the first player to have my name on a Sharks jersey. This is where it all started for me and this place has been so good to me. I've never looked away and I've never taken anything for granted. Even in the dark times off the field, I've never forgotten that it is a massive privilege to wear the Sharks jersey. Every time I pull on the jersey I try to give a performance that is worthy of it. For the Sharks to honour me in the way they have shows that loyalty is a big thing in rugby and I hope it convinces youngsters who are just starting that they can have long careers at only one franchise.

I think of someone like Khuta Mchunu who made his debut as a prop in our first game of the 2019 season against the Sunwolves in Singapore. He has a lot to learn still, but he's hungry and excited to be part of the Sharks family. He has to get more game time, because the only way you can get better as a prop is to play against good opposition. You can't get better on the training field. You can work on certain aspects, but proper game time is the only real way to improve, so I wish Khuta all the best in his career.

Chapter 18

LIFE AFTER RUGBY

I have been working on the transition from being a professional sportsman to venturing into the business world for a few years and, thanks to Wahl Bartmann at Fidelity, I've been given a huge opportunity that I'm really grateful for. I met Wahl seven or eight years ago through rugby – he was a top player himself for both the Sharks and the Springboks. At the time, his kids were big fans of the Beast and they wanted to meet me. Plum used to bring ex-players to hand out the Sharks jerseys and one day he asked Wahl. So Wahl did the jersey thing and then asked me if I would be prepared to have my picture taken with his kids, and of course I was happy to.

Well, that meeting planted a seed and we spoke for a while, then Wahl went away and thought about things and decided that I would be the right fit for his business. He hadn't done a lot of advertising or marketing for Fidelity in the past, so he decided to take me on board as an ambassador. From that initial setup, we did a few adverts and it was going well, so Wahl offered me shares in the business. He wanted to formalise my involvement and that struck a chord for me, because I have this thing deep inside of me that makes me feel like a superhero, always wanting to make people feel safer. So I think security, the Beast and myself provide a lot of good synergies.

I was excited to be part of this huge, prestigious brand and now I was a shareholder and then Wahl thought it would be good to involve me in the day-to-day running of the business. He said he would like to teach me the way the business worked and from there I could start seeing this as my after-rugby plan. So I became a formally enrolled employee at Fidelity; obviously, my rugby career didn't allow me to be there all the time, but when I had the chance I would go to the office and work for Wahl.

He wanted me to start getting used to the environment, talking business to people in the corporate world. I was given the title of clientele manager and my real job was to go out, meet up with clients and make sure they were happy. Most of the time, of course, people just wanted to talk rugby and I was happy to sit and chat, because it's a good ice-breaker. It's easier after that to offer them security products and advice and hopefully it leads to them signing a deal, which can lead to other stuff.

Wahl made the point that this is my time – when I'm in the public eye – to use my platform, because it doesn't last forever. He said that once you're done with your career and the next generation takes over, people forget you very quickly, so you have to make the most of the time you have. So Wahl pushed me and challenged me, and now, seven or eight years down the line, I've learned a lot.

I'm now customer-relations manager and although I have an office in Durban I spend a lot more time in Joburg, shadowing Wahl. When I was injured in 2018 I did my induction and spent a full month in Joburg learning every aspect of the business. It was great to see the way Wahl deals with certain issues and the way he conducts himself. We've become great friends as well as being in business together and he is godfather to my two children. It's quite funny that he managed to persuade me to come hunting with him one day and now it's one of the things I look forward to.

If all goes well, the transition from being a professional rugby player to businessman should go smoothly, but I have reached the stage in my life where I believe it's time to give something back to the game that has given me so much. In the run up to my 100th Test match in 2018 I started a project called 100 Reasons to Dream. Originally it was Ku's idea and it was to try to make a lasting contribution from a significant moment in my career, my 100th cap for the Springboks.

The intention was to give rugby boots to deserving individuals and Asics came on board as a sponsor straight away. I have never forgotten the first time I was given a pair of boots when I was at school and that was the stimulus for the project. I started identifying young kids at schools who didn't have boots, but were inspired to play the game. Then I heard about a ladies' rugby team in the Eastern Cape and gave boots to them, and at the Cape Town Sevens last year I was able to give boots to the Zimbabwe Sevens team.

Originally, the idea was to give away 100 pairs of boots, but it kind of grew and now it's set to get much bigger. There are others out there who want to give more and, through 100 Reasons to Dream, they got excited and wanted to come on board as partners. It's a huge opportunity and we're looking to do even bigger stuff going forward.

I also want to make a difference back home in Zimbabwe. When Robert Mugabe stepped down as president there were parties all over the world and we hoped that things would get better in Zimbabwe, but less than a year later it's as bad as it's ever been. It's tough and it's hard to see how things are ever going to improve there.

Some people in Zimbabwe believe that because I left the country to pursue my dream, I'm a traitor. They think that because I live in South Africa now, I've forgotten where I come from. Well, I've dreamt about being a professional rugby player since I was 16 years old and I couldn't fulfil my dream in Zimbabwe. I had to come to South Africa and I had to work so hard to reach my goal and then I had to work even harder to stay there. I love Zimbabwe and I want to see it come back up again. South Africans who say there are parallels between their country and Zim are wrong. South Africa is a million miles away from Zim.

One of my new goals is to try to make Zimbabwe a rugby power again, one that can make it to a World Cup and compete at that level. I want to establish an academy in Zim, partly because one of the things that led me to South Africa was that there was no professional facility for me in Zim to get the right coaching, nutrition, training, you name it. So my dream is to take what I've learned here and bring it back home. I want to build a great facility, a state-of-the-art academy that can help kids get the right coaching and fulfil their talent, and I've been working towards that goal for the last two years with an organisation called LEAD.

I met a guy through the African Philanthropy Forum, which does a lot of good work in soccer all over Africa. They raise money from wealthy individuals – rich people overseas, top businessmen – who are looking for legitimate ways to give back, and to do it through channels that are not going to use the money for other stuff. So after speaking at one of their meetings and telling them my dream, I've partnered with them. They agreed to try to help me out because it's very much what they do. So I'm hoping that the academy will open its doors in Harare in 2021 and that my dream will come to life.

The idea now is for my academy to take it to the next level. It will be The LEAD Academy and my name will be in there somewhere – we just haven't worked that out yet. I've had politicians approaching me wanting to get involved. Because money just disappears, administration has been the biggest problem for sport in Zimbabwe, but in 2018 government took the bold decision to make Kirsty Coventry the Minister of Sport. Kirsty is a really good friend and that was probably the best decision that's ever been made in the history of sport in Zimbabwe. She's an Olympian, a multiple swimming medallist, someone who can really make a difference in that position. Obviously she has a huge mess to clean up. She's going to have to wipe the sports industry clean because there's a whole lot of people there who just want to grab a piece of the pie and who never contribute anything. So it's a huge job she's taken on and I wish her well. If my schedule allows, I'll be giving her as much support as I can.

In my own small way I'm trying to make a difference. I've started a foundation with one of my really good friends, Kisset Kuda. Although he went to a different school, we've been close since schooldays. Kisset is a very good sports administrator and through us collaborating and forming something of a partnership we've decided to try to make a difference back at home. We set up the Get Involved Foundation a few years ago and, through Kisset's efforts, the organisation does a lot of good work that goes unseen. It has to be under the radar because the way things work back home is that certain folks squash everything good that happens – they don't want the spotlight on people who actually deserve it. They want the spotlight only on themselves and they want all the money that comes into rugby; it's ridiculous.

But Kisset has been working tirelessly to create opportunities for kids who are really talented. Zimbabwe has lots of talent at school-going level; athletics, cricket, rugby, swimming, even basketball, you name it. There's so much, but it just gets lost along the way because there's nothing after school that a kid can aspire to. Kisset has secured sponsorships and scholarships through universities in America, as well as with some clubs in the UK and in South Africa. There are a few guys at the Sharks Academy right now. Kisset's work goes unseen and he does it because he loves it, not because he's looking for praise.

Kisset runs the Foundation from day to day, but he has a finance team and a legal team to help him. We have all the proper structures in place and a lot of the funding comes from the UK. I was in the UK at the end of 2018 and did a launch of the Foundation there in an attempt to get more grants and funding. I had been due to play for the Barbarians that week, but I injured my neck playing against the All Blacks in the Rugby Championship and had to pull out. I didn't want to lose the opportunity to help the Foundation, though, so we did the launch at Saracens Rugby Club in London. A lot of Zimbabweans came along and those were the people we were trying to reach out to – Zimbabweans who can make a difference.

We spoke about what we are doing and teamed up with Cassava, one of the big international cash-remittance companies, based in Britain. The idea is that when people send money home, 10% will be donated by Cassava to the Get Involved Foundation. Cassava is owned by Strive Masiyiwa, who is probably the most successful businessman ever to come out of Zimbabwe. I got to know him a few years ago when I was invited to an all-stars basketball game in South Africa. Strive does amazing work back home and really puts his money to good use.

I've been asked if I will be a tourism ambassador for Zimbabwe, which is a huge honour. They've also asked Danai Gurira from the *Black Panther* movie, who is American, but of Zimbabwean descent. Now the Sharks are playing with the Black Panther branding and it's almost like a childhood fantasy. The movie left a lasting impression on me and filled the gap that has always been there – the absence of black superheroes. The misrepresentation has been resolved and even my kids are talking about Black Panther at home now. It fits well with the Sharks brand, so there's great synergy.

I'm playing with a lot of guys now who will be asking whether they should stay in South Africa and play, or take the money on offer in Europe and Japan. What I've always tried to pass on to the next generation is that you should try to solidify your position here in South Africa before thinking about going overseas.

Stay true to one franchise for as long as possible. Money is always a factor and the attractions of the euro and the pound cannot be denied. Rugby is not a long career and it can be cut short by injuries, but somehow you still have to have faith in the work you are doing, faith that you will be protected and that you'll come back stronger after an injury. A lot of players use the possibility of injury as a scapegoat, but in my opinion it's the wrong way to think.

Trust that God will look after you, dedicate yourself to South Africa, play here for as long as possible, get to 50 Tests, 100 Super Rugby games, and your value will triple and by the time you sign up overseas you will earn way more than if you had gone early in your career. Loyalty is a good thing that teaches you so much and it brings its own reward.

Chapter 19

MY DREAM TEAM

I've been fortunate to have played with and against some of the best rugby players of all time. This is my salute to a few of them. As you'd expect, there are plenty of Sharks in my dream team – eight, in fact – but this is my team and I don't have to please anyone but myself. There's also a Kiwi in there, but since he's one of the legends of the game I'm sure I don't have to make excuses for picking him.

Obviously, there are players I had to leave out that I didn't want to, players like the real hard man, Bakkies Botha, and Butch James, who was a great number 10.

Perhaps aware that he wouldn't make the cut in Beast's team, Butch offers this story as retribution. He says, 'I remember driving from the airport with my brother-in-law and Beast in the car and Beast was on the phone trying to whisper. But for all those who know Beast, he's got the deepest voice in history and he can't whisper. We heard everything because his whisper is as loud as anyone else's normal talking voice.'

188

Jean de Villiers was a real presence at 12, and Willie le Roux is a gifted fullback who is fun to watch. In the forwards I preferred The Hoff, Ryan Kankowski, to Pierre Spies, but Pierre was a great player and Marcell Coetzee might also have made it if he had played longer in this country. The coach of my Dream Team is Dick Muir, the man who made me cry when he told me I was a prop, not a flank, but who stood by me through the tough times. When he said I could play 100 games for the Springboks I thought he was joking, because Dick loves joking, but he wasn't and he was right. So here they are, 15 to 1, the guys I would go to war with.

15 Percy Montgomery

A very interesting character, who we used to call Goldilocks. What I liked most about Percy was that he was a super professional. He was one guy who worked harder than the rest, particularly on his skills to make himself better. He had a great kicking game and was one of the best kickers I've ever played with. He was also a strong defender and achieved a lot in his career.

14 JP Pietersen

JP is an exceptional player, one of the best ever to emerge from the Sharks setup. He was at the Academy at the same time as me, but only for a little while because he went straight from the Under-19s into the Sharks first team. Certainly, the most explosive and aggressive winger I ever played with. In tight games against teams such as the Crusaders in Christchurch you always knew you could rely on JP. Not many guys were brave enough to smash a forward like JP, but he would always take the lead and the forwards would be impressed and motivated as a consequence. We teased him about the fact that he was a lock at school and that he should play in the forwards again, but he used to say he'd had his stint and would never go back there again. He was full of chirps, gave me a difficult time, but I love him to bits and he's one of my closest mates. We still talk every week. He's in France playing for Toulon and has just become a dad to a baby girl, Maya, and he's loving life.

13 Jaque Fourie

With his size and the stuff he did on a rugby field, Jaque was a freak. The best defender I ever played with, who used to run the Springbok defence and had a way of upping the tempo when he was on the field. Whether it was scoring a try or making a big hit, he had a presence that was just immense. And off the field he was the funniest guy I've ever met. He was a joker of note who often played pranks on the coaches and support staff, keeping everyone on their toes. When I first started with the Springboks, our team manager was Arthob Petersen. We were on tour in Wales and we had a team room in the hotel where we ate all our meals. Next to it was a special buffet for VIP guests in the executive suites. Well, Arthob discovered this buffet on day one and he spent his whole week there. We never saw him in the team room at all. Jaque picked up on this and at the team meeting on Friday he stood up and welcomed Arthob to the team, saying, 'We haven't seen you all week. It's nice to have you back.'

12 Frans Steyn

What a talent. When Frans first came on the scene, we'd never seen anything like him. Big, strong, could kick a ball a mile. He could do crazy stuff, play in any position in the backline and make a huge impact. He was so versatile. He sacrificed his Test-match career for the French league. Racing Club offered him a big contract as a young man and he just couldn't turn it down.

11 Bryan Habana

Bryan is the best example I can give of someone who never took anything for granted, particularly when it came to wearing the Springbok jersey. When I first became involved with the Boks, Bryan welcomed me and told me that this was an environment of excellence. He lived that in the way he handled himself on and off the field. You could see the way that he interacted with others and always left a mark. He had family issues behind the scenes that not a lot of people knew about, but he never let that get in the way of performance. In his time he won the IRB Player of the Year and was unquestionably the world's best winger at that time.

10 Morné Steyn

This was a tough decision because I have played with a lot of great flyhalves. Morné was a really talented player and an amazing goal kicker and achieved phenomenal things on the field. My fondest memory of him is the kick to win the series against the British and Irish Lions at Loftus. That was a special day and after that we went on to beat the All Blacks three times in a row and Morné was just on top of his game. What I enjoyed about him was

191

that he was a perfectionist and you knew with Morné in the side that you would always be going forward. He was accurate with his field kicking and always found space behind the defensive line. The press can write what they like about how he limited our play, but in Test-match rugby a flyhalf who kicks his goals and sends you forward is gold.

9 Ruan Pienaar

Ruan is one of the greatest rugby players I ever played with. Like Frans Steyn, he was incredibly versatile, could play 10 and 15 and excelled in other positions as well, but at number 9 he was closer to the action and dynamic with the ball in hand. He was a great passer of the ball; his passes were always spot on and no one ever complained that they were too low or too high. He was deceptively quick too. It didn't look like he was moving fast, but he could slice through a gap, go round a wing and score a try. Then he could convert it from the edge of the field, just like he did that day when we beat the Crusaders at Kings Park.

8 Ryan Kankowski

We used to call him The Hoff, after David Hasselhoff, the guy on *Baywatch* [and years before, on *Knight Rider*]. At his best when he first came onto the scene, Ryan was a powerful number 8 who was full of speed. He could turn a game around with his pace. I remember a couple of times when he rounded wingers and scored tries to get us on the front foot. We were at the Academy together when I first got to play alongside him and he really benefited from playing Sevens for the Blitzbokke. His speed and skills improved hugely as a result. He could have played a lot more Test rugby, but he didn't really suit the style Springbok rugby is known for.

7 Richie McCaw (Captain)

The only overseas player in my side is also my captain, because he was a phenomenal leader who didn't need words – he led by example. Off the field, he was a true gentleman, and most of the time I was scared to talk to him or even approach him. When I was a kid I used to idolise Richie because back then I played in the back row and when I got to play against him I had to pinch myself to make sure I wasn't dreaming. Richie was just a freak; his work rate was crazy, making 30 tackles a game, being involved in so many breakdowns, scoring a try or two and never getting tired. Just a hard man. We got stuck into him so many times and so many teams targeted him, but he could have a broken nose, broken ribs, concussion, and he'd just carry on playing because he was as tough as nails. Without doubt, the toughest player I ever played against.

6 Schalk Burger

Truly something special. With the ball in hand, Schalk was incredibly destructive, yet he could also link between the forwards and the backs and, as a result, he created a lot of tries and scored plenty as well. A devastating defender and the epitome of a dynamic loose forward. Good guitarist too.

5 Victor Matfield

The best lineout man I ever played with or against. His special skill was working out the opposition lineout in real time. He would call us together and tell us they were going to do this or that and, sure enough, that's what would happen and we would get the ball. What you are looking for from a number 5 lock is good lineout ball; other stuff is just a bonus. Off the field, Victor was a little distant. He had a presence and he didn't particularly like speaking English. It was quite hard to get into his good books or to get a conversation going with him. It was difficult for me and maybe a few other youngsters, because he put himself on a pedestal, but you put up with that because of what he gave you on the field. You knew who was in charge and if you got something wrong he would come down on you like a ton of bricks. You didn't want to get anything wrong in that lineout because he put the fear of God into you. I lifted him a lot and I learned to make sure I got everything right, because if I didn't, at the Monday video review he would get stuck into me properly and I'd feel as small as a mouse.

4 Eben Etzebeth

One of the best, most explosive second rowers I have ever played with. He brings another level of physicality on the field and I would rather have him on my side than against me. A great friend, we get along really well on and off the field. He is a good lad with a big heart and when he scrums behind you there is only one way, and that's forward.

3 Jannie du Plessis

The Doc. One of the best tightheads and a real anchor in the scrum. A lot of the work Jannie did went unseen, but he would give us those solid right shoulders when we needed them and never shirked the hard work. They always say the most important player in any team is the tighthead and Jannie was proof of that. He did a great job there for many years for the Sharks and the one thing I really liked about him was his consistency. You knew what you were gonna get from Jannie and he'd smash guys in the tackle, hit rucks, and although he didn't carry a lot he would do those hard yards up front, the 'ugly work', so to speak. A leader in his own right who had a knack of saying the right thing at the right time, not just to the players, but to the ref as well! His dedication was something else, because as a doctor he ran a full-time general practice at the same time as being a professional rugby player. His mum was the pillar of strength in her boys' lives and when their dad got sick she took on the disciplinary role. The boys would make sure Dad was there at big games and we would all chat to him and have pictures taken, and one thing that was really evident was that their dad meant the world to them. They would get really emotional when he was at the stadium to watch them play.

2 Bismarck du Plessis

Bizzy was a huge presence on the field. The secret to his success was hard work. In the gym he always pushed me. Often, when I was ready to take it easy or take a breather, he would be on my case saying, 'Beast, let's go. Let's do extra, let's work harder because nothing comes easy.' And on the field it was the same; if I stepped off the gas, he'd be the constant voice in my head pushing me to keep going. At his peak, he was the world's best hooker and stronger than anyone I ever played with. He was able to do freaky stuff and you could be up against the All Blacks at Eden Park, but

195

he would get his head into a ruck and win the ball from five other guys. His physical presence on the field was second to none.

1 Tendai Mtawarira/Os du Randt

It's my team so I get to play, but I'm not going to blow smoke up myself, so I nominate Os. I played against him in his last season with the Cheetahs and took his place in the Springbok team when he retired. I appreciated Os's longevity and the fact that he played a tough position all that time. A powerful scrummager, good tackler, and a carrier all over the field with a solid presence at the set-piece. It's testimony to the kind of person he was that he could do all of that and win two World Cups.

Many of the players in my Dream Team walked the hard road with me and I'm grateful to all of them. I've learned some tough lessons, but I have no regrets. For those who want to make a career of rugby, remember that it takes a lot of hard work to stay at the top. There's always going to be someone breathing down your neck, trying to take your place, so make sure you stay focused and stay hungry. Write down your goals and read them each day. If you read them out loud, you speak them into existence.

ACKNOWLEDGEMENTS

First of all, I have to thank Beast for giving his time so generously during the busiest season of his career. He was being pulled in half a dozen different directions at once, but somehow we squeezed in enough face time to make this book possible.

Thanks to Andrea Nattrass at Pan Macmillan, who never seemed to worry how far behind schedule I was and had faith from day one in my ability to deliver the final product. Thanks also to my editor, Sean Fraser, who battled load-shedding and oxymorons in making the text come alive.

Thanks to Steve Haag, the indefatigable photographer, who made 15 years of his Beast images available and then took hundreds more, including the beautiful ones that adorn the front and back covers.

Thanks to Thato Monale at SuperSport, who was kind enough to book me as a commentator on many Sharks games during the writing process. Being inside the citadel made it a lot easier to connect with the relevant people to bring Beast's story to life. Thanks also to Sean Everett at SuperSport, the inspiration behind the final chapter of this book.

Thanks to Beast's family, Felix and Bertha Mtawarira, and particularly his lovely wife, Ku, who opened her home to me and made sure that Beast was in the right place at the right time.

Thanks, too, to all those who helped to tell the story, particularly Paul Davies, the rugby master at Peterhouse when Beast was there. And to the other Paul Davis, a teacher at Peterhouse at the same time, who explained the anomaly and kindly put me in touch with the right man.

Thanks to Dick Muir, an old friend who has something in common with me as the father of a daughter who rides very expensive horses. It can truly be said that this book would not exist without Dick, who saw Beast's potential and had the wit to point it in the right direction.

Thanks to all the former players who so generously shared their memories of Beast, particularly John Smit, Butch James, Jean de Villiers and Odwa Ndungane. And special thanks to Regan Hoskins, a thoroughly decent man.

And finally, thanks to my family, Rhian and Elinor, who had to do extra work on the farm to allow me the time to write this book.

Lots of love and all the Beast ... I mean 'the best'.

INDEX